Patinas of Life
Patrick Wood

Copyright © by Patrick Wood, 2025

All rights reserved.

Works in this book were previously published, in slightly different versions, in *Press Times* print and digital editions.

ISBN: 979-8-9938316-1-9

Printed, bound, and distributed by IngramSpark

Cover and interior design by Caleigh Cleary

Project management and copyediting services by Tiffany Jablonowski, Alena Schuessler, and Chloe Smith

Book design, editorial, and proofreading services provided by Hard-Penned Press
an imprint of The Teaching Press at UW-Green Bay
A student-powered, community-serving publisher and printer
in Northeastern Wisconsin
University of Wisconsin-Green Bay
2420 Nicolet Drive, Green Bay, Wisconsin 54311-7001

✉ teachingpress@uwgb.edu   📷 @theteachingpress

🌐 blog.uwgb.edu/teaching-press

Also by Patrick Wood

Tapestry of Love and Loss

Dear Reader

Reflections

Dedication

To Mary, my cherished companion on all of life's trails, and to our daughters and their beloveds—Margaret and Michael, Anne and David, Katelyn and Ryan—whose own journeys have added such rich texture to our shared story. And to our grandchildren—Dylan, James, Rory, Patrick, Michael, Shannon, and Maddie—who remind us daily that the most beautiful patinas come not from weathering alone, but from the love that binds us, generation to generation, in this ever-evolving tapestry of belonging.

Table of Contents

vii	Dedication
15	Introduction
17	Going Back, Going Forward
18	Cast a Long Shadow
19	The Cloak of Deterioration
20	Amity
21	A Journey to Peru
22	Why Do We Fall in Love?
23	Driving the Body Hard
24	Are We the Hope or the Despair?
25	What Matters?
26	Get Up and Ride (or Walk) the Camino
28	Imagination Hour Revisited
29	Dream Avatars: Navigating the Uncharted Realms of Self
31	Journey Across Time: Exploring the Morality and Possibilities of Time Travel
33	Embracing Agape Love: A Foundation for Lasting Connections
35	The Essence of Accumulation: Sharing Makes It Meaningful
36	Paradigm Shift for A Day
37	The Wind Down
38	Measurements of Being
39	Why It Matters
40	The Subtle Touch
41	Navigating the Terrain of Relationships: Lover versus Companion
42	Crossing Continuums
43	The Bygone
44	The Vanishing Legacy
46	When Autumn Comes
47	The Journey Over the Destination

48	A Glimpse into Tragedy
49	The Unasked Question
50	The Elusive Quest for Eternal Youth: Reflections on the Fountain of Youth
51	Deus Ex Machina
52	A Poetic Insight: Ready for Perils
53	Unveiling the Echoes of Time in Shelley's "Ozymandias"
55	Chasing Ghosts of the Past: A Reflection
57	Ephemeral Echoes
59	Joy and Sorrow
60	Embracing Stoicism
61	Blueprint for the End of Days
62	The Ebb and Flow of Love
64	The Transitory Tapestry of Love
66	The Saints in Our Midst
67	"To Thine Own Self Be True"
69	The True Measure of Success
71	Unrequited Love: A Timeless Muse in Poetry
73	On Composite Selves
74	The Cost of Estrangement
76	On Aging
77	Reaching Beyond the Veil
79	Celebrating the Visionaries Among Us
80	The Power of a Name
81	Becoming Instruments of God's Peace
83	Not Them. Us.
85	Finding the Perfect Someone
86	We Are One
87	The Gift of Life and The Inevitable Abyss
88	The Games We Play: Timewasters or Strategic Tools
89	The Human Condition and Its Many Variations
90	The Better Half
91	Grave Thoughts From the Graveyard
92	Reconciling the Existence of God with the Concept of Faith
93	The Body Electric: Our Brief Dance on Earth
95	Autumn Leaves
96	Integrating the Shadows and Ghosts
97	Human Body Design
98	What is Truly Important in Life?
99	The Implications of Telling a Lie

100	Protected Moments in Time: A Reflection on Love and Change
101	Looking Past; Looking Forward
103	Little Bursts of Happiness
104	Intersections, Engagements, and Disruptions
105	Wish I Was an Angel
106	The Inside In or the Outside Out
107	On Aging and Invisibility
108	The Fragility of Life
109	Current Spaces and Empty Chairs
111	Humans Playing Humans
112	Life's Meaning
113	The Many Faces of Love
115	Golden Friends
116	Moving Beyond a Transactional Life
117	Flowers on the Grave
118	The Complex Beauty of a Flower
119	The Pursuit of Relevance
120	The Art of Influence
121	Memories of Yesteryear
122	Unto Dust
124	On Being an Introvert or an Extrovert
125	The Batons
126	Guardian Angels Among Us
128	The Arrival or the Journey
129	The Wealth Divide
130	Whispers in the Wind
132	Private Universes
134	Amplification of Individuality Through Conductivity of the Whole
136	If You Could Time Travel…
138	Beyond a Crossroads Where Knowledge Meets Experience
140	On True Love
142	Coming Full Circle: From Camp II to Family Legacy
145	Love and Quantum Entanglement; Hearts Across the Universe
147	The Real Threat Isn't from Space
148	On Our Own
149	The Museum of Our Lives
151	Timeless Virtues in Changing Times

Page	Title
153	Life's Constraints: Maximum Intensity versus Duration
155	Finding Common Ground: What We All Share as Americans
157	The Leadership Void: When Those at the Helm Fall, We Must Rise–Peacefully
158	Finding What We're Planted Here to Give
159	Mind Erasures
161	When Forever Changes in a Single Goodbye
163	Serving Others, Finding Ourselves
165	The Fading Echo of High School Hearts
167	Why We Are Here: A Public Discourse
169	The Difference We Make: Finding Purpose in our Finite Time
171	Coming Home
173	The Hidden Victory in Losing
175	The Continuum of Life: Making a Difference at Every Stage
177	Different Strokes for Different Retirements
179	A Moment in Time in Cartagena
180	Music's Magical Imprint
182	The Art of Joie de Vivre: When Joy Becomes the Journey
183	Speedy vs Steady
185	Finding the Sacred Within the Mundane
187	The Dash Between the Years
189	The Geography of Jealousy: What Age Teaches Us About Love
191	Lonesome: The Word Nobody Wants to Claim
193	Visiting with Ghosts

Introduction

Life leaves its mark on everything it touches.

Walk through any ancient city and you'll witness this truth written in bronze and stone. The copper dome that once gleamed like fire now wears a crown of verdigris. The marble steps, polished smooth by countless footfalls, tell stories in their worn grooves. The silver chalice bears the lustrous tarnish of centuries, each oxidized layer a testament to hands that held it, lips that blessed it, moments that transformed it.

We are no different.

Just as metals acquire their patinas through time and exposure, we too develop the beautiful markings of experience. Our lives accumulate layers of wisdom earned through trial, scars that map our journeys, and the rich oxidation that comes only from a life fully engaged with the world. These patinas don't diminish us—they define us. They are the proof that we have not merely existed but truly lived.

Yet, unlike the predictable chemistry of copper meeting air, our human patinas form through something far more complex: the alchemy of choice, relationship, loss, discovery, and growth. Each decision leaves its trace. Every relationship weathers us in ways both gentle and profound. Our dreams develop their own unique finish as they meet reality, creating surfaces more beautiful than we could have imagined in their original, untested state.

The patina process is not always comfortable. When oxidation burns, when weathering feels overwhelming, when the very foundations of who we thought we were seem to shift beneath our feet, we may long for the simplicity of our earlier, unadorned selves. But transformation demands its due. The most magnificent patinas emerge not from gentle exposure, but from the storms that strip away the superficial and reveal what lies beneath.

This book contains observations and insights gathered from one person's examination of how life marks us. Some pieces may resonate with your experience; others may feel foreign or irrelevant. Take what serves you and leave what doesn't. These are not universal truths, but particular reflections on the patina process as I've witnessed and lived it.

The passages that follow explore different surfaces of human experience—some weathered smooth, others bearing the sharp edges of recent impact.

The surface is just the beginning.

Going Back, Going Forward

In the realm of passing time, where the currents of life have flowed relentlessly, traversing beneath the sturdy arches of many bridges, one finds oneself unable to retrace their steps. Such is the nature of our journey, where the exuberance of youth and the aspirations of an uncharted future paint vivid images in our minds, far grander than the stark realities we face each day.

As the years have stretched on, extending far beyond the reach of any remaining vitality, the ties that once bound us to those who embarked on divergent paths have faded into little significance. Life passed by without sporadic check-ins to refresh the bonds of friendship and love. Each of us chose roads untraveled by the other, rendering us unrecognizable if we were to chance upon one another in some gathering or occasion.

After a prolonged absence from someone we once held dear, the very essence of that connection transforms, even if fragments of memories linger on. One can't go back in time because life evolves in stages—stages that fit uniquely with an individual's aging process.

Cast a Long Shadow

We all walk through life with a shadow. Our shadow follows us wherever we go. It is visible in semi-darkness and invisible in the stark light of day.

In some regards, it is an avatar of sorts that is always there whether one sees it or not. In dusk the silhouette becomes more elongated perhaps knowing that the day is ending. It stretches to its fullest potential, a silent inspiration for us to always be reaching for, stretching to those stars.

The Cloak of Deterioration

As we age, we often conceal certain truths. We put on a facade of strength and control, pretending that nothing has changed and everything remains the same. In our attempts to deceive ourselves and others, we go to great lengths, but time inevitably strips away our illusions.

Time patiently waits until we are but a mere shadow of our former selves. We are exposed as vulnerable, reminiscent of a helpless newborn relying entirely on others for survival. Simple tasks like feeding ourselves become challenging, distinguishing between days blurs, and we fixate on trivialities like ice cream. We stumble. Gradually, we descend further into the depths, arrogantly believing that this fate could never befall us.

This reality cannot be evaded. It is an inescapable part of the human experience that as we live longer, our bodies will eventually betray us. However, with preparation, we can alleviate the burden on those close to us. Even in our diminished state, we can leave behind an untarnished legacy of accomplishments.

Amity

There is a certain amount of joy in reuniting with a group of old friends to reminisce about cherished memories while also creating new ones together. We emphasize the value of friendship, the power of shared experiences, and the warmth of nostalgia.

There is an excitement of gathering with these familiar faces, recounting past adventures, and laughing over shared stories. These encounters, however frequent, provide a sense of comfort and belonging, as they bring back memories from earlier days, reminding everyone of the bonds with the passage of time and the changes that life brings. The connections formed with old friends remain enduring and special and enrich the bond further.

So, cherish your friendships, celebrate the past, and seize opportunities to make new memories with those who have been a part of your lives for a long time. It serves as a heartwarming reminder of the value of friendship and the joy of sharing moments with the people we care about.

A Journey to Peru

This is a story of a missionary, a mission, a family, and a community of learners.

Sister Marie Esterre was a devoted nun of the Sisters of St. Joseph of Carondelet in St. Paul, Minnesota. In the late 1960s, she became the Mother Superior of the order's congregation in Arequipa, Peru. Sr. Marie also was my aunt. During a visit to our family in the States, she and Frank Wood, my father, collaborated with St. Norbert College to create a program for St. Norbert students to teach and study at La Universidad de Santa Maria in Arequipa while living with Peruvian families. Dad led seven students to Arequipa in the program's first year in 1970, accompanied by our entire family of eight children. Tom and Luci Phelan guided the students in 1971, and Richard and Mechtilde Calnin helmed the program in 1972.

Nowadays "study abroad" programs are an established feature in higher education; back then, they were a rarity, and St. Norbert was charting a course through a seldom-traveled wilderness. For many of the students, the journey to Peru marked their first exposure to a different culture, leaving them forever changed and connected to people, places, and history.

The instability of the Peruvian economy under the dictatorship of Juan Velasco Alvarado posed difficulties that ultimately became insurmountable. At one point in 1971, the program participants were trapped in Peru after Aerolíneas Peruanas, the airline they were counting on to bring them home, went bankrupt. Ultimately, the third year was also the last year because of the increasingly volatile political climate. Nevertheless, it was a remarkable experiment that paved the way for St. Norbert College's international study programs today.

Visiting a foreign culture with both differences and shared virtues can profoundly impact individuals. Years later, a Peruvian Reunion at St. Norbert College honored Professors Wood, Phelan, Calnin, and their spouses for blazing the trail for future learners with the installation of ceremonial benches in a prominent location on campus. This fitting memorial will remind all who participated to cherish those special moments from long ago.

Why Do We Fall in Love?

Humans fall in love due to a combination of biological, psychological, and social factors. Love is a complex emotion that helps with forming strong emotional connections, fostering relationships, and bonding between individuals. It involves the release of various hormones, such as dopamine, oxytocin, and serotonin, which contribute to feelings of pleasure, attachment, and intimacy. Personal experiences, cultural influences, and shared interests also play a significant role in shaping how and why people fall in love.

But falling in love, really, was it the first dance, the first kiss, the first time a glance with a smile went our way? And then what?

Does love promise a wonderful world together?

Does love promise a beautiful set of children?

Does love promise every day together spent as a holiday?

Does love promise a together forever and hereafter?

These are not promised, only hoped for.

Driving the Body Hard

We all take life at a certain pace. Some are chill and let it happen. Others are more deliberate and plan it all out. And then, there are those that are riding the winds and tackling the storms with only the illusion of fear. Based on those options, life can be long, much longer, or possibly a little shorter.

There isn't any way to judge which is the better choice because we all punch out eventually at the end of the trail. So, the question is, do you want to cross over to the other side pristine and completely intact? Or do you want to leave everything on the field, from nose to toes? Maybe it depends on what you're trying to do–accomplish some good things or hang out and watch the world go by. Your call.

Are We the Hope or the Despair?

As parents, we want to give our children a happy childhood. We want them to be introduced to the world in a beautiful and truthful way. In fact, one of the greatest gifts that parents can give their children is a happy childhood.

We want our children to grow up with compassion. We want our children to grow up loving the people in the world around us. We want them to have compassion in their hearts for our fellow man. Some of our children make it that way and some don't.

Those that don't may end up with violence in their hearts. And as Isaac Asimov once wrote, "Violence is the last refuge of the incompetent."

At some point, can't we as adults grow up and act as inspirations for our children and the next generation—rather than showing them the wreckage and violence in the world, the lack of respect, and the disregard for another point of view that is out there right now?

What Matters?

Remember those events back in high school—sports, homecoming, prom, the musical? It was a big deal back then. And now?

Remember those happenings back in college—football games, parties, concerts, road trips? More big deals back in the day. And now?

You ran the gauntlet of life with all the challenges, barriers, and naysayers. So, here you are. At last, you can recalibrate from this place and time you have gotten to and move forward, with the realization that the big stuff from once-upon-a-time is now minuscule. It no longer even exists, except in memory. Why? Because in a world of rational perspective and the ability to take the long view, things take on their proper significance—or insignificance.

But there are eternal values that we can touch, if only briefly. There can be joy in every moment if we so choose. It is joy that makes any single instant into an eternal experience of love.

Get Up and Ride (or Walk) the Camino

The Camino de Santiago, also known as the Way of St. James, has a history that spans over a thousand years. Its origins are rooted in the early 9th century, when the tomb of Saint James was miraculously discovered in what is now the city of Santiago de Compostela in northwest Spain.

The discovery of the apostle's remains turned the site into a major Christian pilgrimage destination, rivaling even Jerusalem and Rome. Pilgrims from all over Europe began making their way to Santiago, and the routes leading to the shrine gradually formed what we now know as the Camino.

During the Middle Ages, the Camino de Santiago became a well-established network of trails and roads. The pilgrimage was a profound spiritual journey, offering penance and the opportunity to seek forgiveness. It also served as a cultural exchange route, with pilgrims sharing stories, music, and art, contributing to the spread of knowledge and ideas across Europe.

In the 19th and 20th centuries, the Camino saw a decline in popularity, partly due to political turmoil in Spain and changes in religious practices. However, the pilgrimage experienced a revival in the late 20th century, largely driven by a renewed interest in spirituality, adventure, and a desire to connect with history and culture.

Today, the Camino de Santiago has regained its status as one of the world's most famous pilgrimages. It offers a range of routes, each with its unique charm, from the rugged Camino Francés to the coastal Camino del Norte. Pilgrims, whether driven by faith or a desire for self-discovery, continue to walk or cycle these ancient paths, forging new traditions while honoring the rich history that underlies this remarkable journey.

I walked the Camino eight years ago, which was a pilgrimage to remember having hiked coming up from Portugal in the south. Recently, my cousins Jimmy and Marty rode their bikes from Pamplona to Santiago. I met them with a car and was able to help with their luggage and gear towards the end of their pilgrimage. It was glorious to film those guys riding into the front of the Basilica after their arduous trek on the road. We especially savored the brotherhood of bonding at Mass that Sunday as the last people who were able to enter with hundreds left outside to possibly catch it another time. "Buen Camino," it was!

Imagination Hour Revisited

Sunday when our three girls were young, we held "Imagination Hour." We used this hour to "imagine" and come up with new and innovative things in brainstorming sessions.

Back in the day, we came up with a reversible cape concept and called it "HatCapers–Great Adventures with the Flip of a Cape." We thought of a frog turning into a prince; a Cinderella to a princess and the list went on.

For the heck of it, I shopped them around and was able to get a sewing license with McCalls and then a license from Whimsicality costumes. Then, the Boston Museum asked us to design two additions to the line to add to their catalog–a knight to a dragon, and a white rabbit to Alice in Wonderland.

One of the best gifts parents can give to their children is the ability to imagine and dream, knowing that anything is possible, if minds are set for it. Besides having those hours of quality time with the family, we had a lot of fun creating stuff and just making dreams come true.

Dream Avatars: Navigating the Uncharted Realms of Self

In the realm of dreams, a fascinating phenomenon unfolds—our dream avatars, alternate expressions of ourselves, embark on extraordinary adventures. As we sleep, these avatars traverse uncharted landscapes with friends and acquaintances, weaving tales that linger in our waking consciousness.

Consider the notion that each nocturnal escapade contributes to the richness of our being. The dream avatar, a vessel of our desires and subconscious whispers, returns with memories that transcend the boundaries of the dream world. These experiences, though born in the realm of slumber, leave an indelible mark on our waking selves.

Imagine a night where your dream avatar engages in a grand adventure, surrounded by familiar faces and unknown landscapes. The emotions felt during these dream exploits linger upon waking, infusing your reality with a newfound sense of fulfillment. It's as if your dream self has unlocked hidden dimensions within you, enriching the tapestry of your existence.

Exploring this concept further, one can't help but wonder how these dream avatars shape our identities over time. Could they serve as a reservoir of untapped potential, influencing our choices and perspectives as we navigate the waking world? Perhaps, in the silent hours of the night, we are not merely passive observers of our dreams but active participants in the ongoing narrative of self-discovery.

Dream avatars, with their ephemeral existence, beckon us to question the boundaries between the conscious and the subconscious. What if the lessons learned and memories forged in the dream realm are not confined to the night but seep into the daylight, altering our perception of reality?

As we delve into the enigma of dream avatars, we find ourselves standing at the intersection of who we were, who we are, and who we aspire to become. The dream world becomes a canvas where the threads of our past, present, and future are woven together, creating a tapestry of enriched life experiences.

In embracing the concept of dream avatars, we invite a profound exploration of the self that transcends the limitations of waking existence.

For in the dance between dreams and reality, we discover that our nocturnal odysseys are not mere escapades but transformative journeys that help mold us into the architects of our destiny.

Journey Across Time: Exploring the Morality and Possibilities of Time Travel

In the ever-expanding realm of human curiosity, the notion of time travel has captivated minds for centuries. The desire to revisit moments with loved ones who've departed or to catch a glimpse of the unfolding future ignites the imagination. However, delving into the prospect of time travel reveals a tapestry woven with moral, ethical, and economical complexities.

The allure of reconnecting with those who've left us is undeniably powerful. Imagine the chance to spend an afternoon with departed friends and family, catching up on the chapters of life that unfolded after their departure. It's a sentiment many share, and it speaks to the profound impact relationships have on the human experience.

Yet, as we ponder the prospect of navigating the corridors of time, ethical questions arise. Would we disrupt the natural order of events? Could altering the past inadvertently reshape the present and future? The delicate balance between nostalgia and the potential repercussions of tampering with time demands careful consideration.

Looking forward poses its own set of challenges. The unknown future, a realm of infinite possibilities, sparks both excitement and trepidation. Peering into what lies ahead holds the potential to shape our decisions in the present, but it also raises questions about free will and the consequences of knowing too much.

While the concept of time travel may seem confined to the realms of science fiction, theories and speculations from brilliant minds like Einstein hint at the tantalizing possibility. However, the practicality of such journeys remains elusive, reminding us that for now, reliving the past remains an unattainable dream—one that can only be realized in a memory and not in reality.

As we grapple with these hypotheticals, it's essential to consider not just the question of "can we," but also the "should we." If time travel becomes a reality, navigating its implications will require a thoughtful approach. Who decides the rules? How do we safeguard against unintended consequences?

In the face of these complexities, one truth remains: The past, present, and future are intricately interconnected. As we dream of conversations with historical giants and glimpses into the years that lie ahead, the ethical responsibility accompanying such endeavors cannot be ignored.

So, while we may not have unlocked the secrets of time travel–yet–the mere contemplation of its possibilities invites us to reflect on our past, make mindful choices in the present, and approach the future with a sense of wonder and responsibility.

Embracing Agape Love: A Foundation for Lasting Connections

In the tapestry of human relationships, the thread of love weaves through the fabric of our lives, creating bonds that withstand the tests of time and adversity. At the heart of these connections lies a profound concept: agape love.

Agape love, often described as selfless and unconditional, transcends the ordinary boundaries of affection. Its roots delve deep into the core of our humanity, influencing the dynamics of marriage, friendship, and community.

Agape Love in Marriage

Marriage, an institution built on the pillars of commitment and companionship, flourishes when adorned with the mantle of agape love. In the face of trials, agape love stands resilient, a beacon guiding spouses through the ebb and flow of life. It is the choice to prioritize the well-being of a partner over personal desires, fostering an environment where sacrificial love becomes the cornerstone of a lasting union.

Agape Love in Friendship

In the realm of friendship, agape love transforms casual companionship into a force that transcends circumstances. True friends are those who embrace each other's imperfections, standing by one another through thick and thin. Agape love fosters an environment where friends become a source of unwavering support, demonstrating a selflessness that mirrors the divine. Rudyard Kipling's poem "The Thousandth Man" paints a vivid portrait of agape friendship.

Agape Love in the Community

Communities thrive when agape love becomes the lifeblood that courses through the veins of shared experiences. It is the embodiment of compassion and empathy that binds individuals together, creating a foundation of diverse yet interconnected lives. In times of need, agape love compels community members to extend a helping hand, embodying the essence of "love thy neighbor."

The Divine Thread

From a Christian perspective, agape love finds its roots in the divine. Many believe that God's love for humanity is the epitome of selfless, sacrificial love—the very essence of agape. Understanding and embodying this divine love can serve as a compass, guiding individuals, couples, and communities toward stronger, more meaningful connections.

As we navigate the intricate landscapes of marriage, friendship, and community, let us embrace the transformative power of agape love. In doing so, we contribute to a world where the bonds we forge are not easily broken–a testament to the enduring strength of selfless, unconditional love.

The Essence of Accumulation: Sharing Makes it Meaningful

In a world where we amass treasures and experiences, let's not forget the profound truth—accumulation gains its true value when shared with others. Material possessions and achievements may fill our lives, but without someone to share them with, the joy they bring remains incomplete.

So, let's embrace the beauty of sharing, for it is in those shared moments that our accumulations find their true purpose and meaning.

Paradigm Shift for a Day

Going off the grid for a day can provide a balance between productivity and self-regeneration. It offers a chance to disconnect, focus on non-digital activities, and foster mindfulness. While challenging, it's still possible and can be a valuable reset in our increasingly digital lives.

Taking a day off the grid allows you to break the constant digital connectivity, reducing stress and promoting mental well-being. It creates space for activities like reading, outdoor pursuits, or face-to-face interactions, fostering a sense of presence and relaxation. Productivity may decrease in traditional terms, yet the mental recharge gained often leads to increased overall effectiveness in the long run.

The Wind Down

We all become addicted to time. We become more addicted the older we get. Hanging on and savoring the gift of another day is not another given, so we push into it with a little more heart.

Recently, I attended a funeral. The life lived was long—linked with many beautiful times and people joined along the way. She had pressed the world hard for all the juices each day would give up. Those who were there were heart-filled with joy and celebration. A tinge of sadness hung subtly in the air, but the vision of spirituality shined brightly ahead.

The joy outweighed the grief knowing the ethereal paths ahead were ones of eternity where down the line we'll all be together again… He truly is a loving God.

Measurements of Being

Exploring success in life involves a nuanced perspective. While financial achievements like money, assets, and material possessions are conventional measures, the spiritual dimension—encompassing service, noble purpose, and positive impact on the world—adds profound depth to the concept of success.

The balance between material and spiritual fulfillment often shapes a more comprehensive view of a successful life.

Why it Matters

Pursuing fame and acclaim has been a long-standing desire, regardless of the avenue—whether it be academics, sports, or any other endeavor.

Unexpectedly finding success in an unanticipated field prompts reflection on the significance of any such recognition of this field or the others. While being acknowledged by faceless strangers may briefly satisfy the ego, the transient nature of their attention underscores the insignificance of external validation.

In the end, true fulfillment lies not in the fleeting acknowledgment of others, but in the pursuit of personal growth and fulfillment for the ultimate good.

The Subtle Touch

In the course of daily living, we all experience subtle touches from those around us. Somebody says something, somebody else says another thing, and then the conversation continues on and on.

I feel this strongly when I spend time with my grandchildren. They are young and don't have the disruptions and distractions of the world yet. They are just being who they are, innocently loving everyone that graces their presence on one day, followed by another, followed by yet another. We can wonder where this blend of soul comes from—is it a part of this world or some other place?

These subtle touches are needed in this world to bring greater civility and love to us all.

Navigating the Terrain of Relationships: Lover versus Companion

In the intricate tapestry of human connections, the distinction between having a lover and having a companion carries profound implications. A lover embodies the fervor of fleeting moments, characterized by fervent passion and exhilarating unpredictability. Conversely, a companion epitomizes a steadfast presence, offering solace, stability, and a sense of home.

The allure of a lover lies in the intoxicating dance of emotions, the fiery intensity that ignites the soul. Yet, it is often accompanied by the looming shadows of uncertainty, leaving one teetering on the edge of exhilaration and apprehension. In contrast, a companion exudes the warmth of familiarity, a sanctuary where vulnerability is embraced and fears are assuaged.

However, the demarcation between these roles is not rigid; rather, it is fluid, subject to the whims of individual preferences and evolving circumstances. What one seeks in a lover during the throes of passion may differ from the companionship yearned for in moments of solitude.

Ultimately, the essence of fulfillment in relationships lies in striking a harmonious balance between the ardor of a lover and the solace of a companion. It is in this equilibrium that one discovers the true essence of companionship–a union where passion intertwines with security, and love blossoms in its myriad forms.

Crossing Continuums

A fact of life is that as soon as we are born, we begin the brief or lengthy process of dying. No time is a "just right" time for death because of the many complex variables of living starting with the humanity around us.

I once knew a number of people who ran life in the fast lane. They ran hard. They accomplished a lot. And then boom! It was over, just like that. A heart attack. Cancer. Here and then gone in a few minutes, a few weeks, or a few months. If it wasn't immediately, it would be one sort of problem that cascades into another and then another. No one expects it. Fate steps boldly and dispassionately in; Fate is deaf to any brand of supplication. Prayers generally ameliorate yet don't affect the outcome.

Each believed that they had so much more to do, so much more of life ahead of them. Not so. Sadness and disappointment barged in because there was so much more to do (or so they thought). And yet, these untimely, hard stops were meant to be, for reasons no one has ever explained well. The hills ahead and the mountains behind falsely summoned–not knowing that the climbing can, as in so many cases, abruptly end. And then, we are left with a legacy of what we have done with others remaining to witness and judge.

Perhaps it doesn't have to be what I've described above. We can make short-term plans for the foreseeable trails ahead. We can make the long plans, that may or may not happen, with low expectations. In a way, our past accomplishments are banked as a foundational legacy. The hopes and dreams which hopefully materialize beyond that can be icing on the cake if they are realized.

Being ready for the inevitable crossing over to the continuum of spiritual infinity makes us feel confident in what was done in our wake. The present and future are bonus deeds we garner as we try to live as beings with purpose–the noble purpose of doing good before departing, secure in the knowledge that what we left in the continuum of physical finitude has made it a better place.

The Bygone

As I stroll down memory lane, I am enveloped in a wistful nostalgia for the bygone days. Those were the days when our hearts brimmed with youthful exuberance, and our friendships were pure, untouched by the transactional nature of today's world. We were united not by wealth or status, but by the simple joy of being together.

In those days, we were all just scraping by, but our spirits were rich with hope and optimism. We didn't need material possessions to define our worth; our worth was measured by the depth of our connections and the richness of our relationships.

Looking back now, with the wisdom of hindsight, there are few regrets. We realize that those fleeting moments of laughter and camaraderie were the true treasures of our youth. We yearn for the days when time seemed to stand still, when the future stretched out before us like an endless road, full of promise and possibility.

But alas, nothing lasts forever. Life moves on, carrying us along with it, and the innocence of youth slips away, leaving behind only memories and echoes of the past. Yet, amid the bittersweet longing for what once was, there remains a glimmer–a hope that we can still find gladness and possibly elation in the moments that lie ahead.

So let us savor each day as it comes, holding onto the memories of the past while embracing the beauties of the future. For in the end, it is not the wealth we amass or the possessions we acquire that truly matter, but the love we share and the memories we create along the way.

The Vanishing Legacy

Every day people do things they deem important—or that someone else deems important. Like ants working steadily, they move through routines that feel essential in the moment. When one looks back at all the work—corporate analyses and presentations, small business ventures built from scratch, physical labor like collecting garbage each week, entrepreneurial dreams pursued in garages and storefronts—really, what was it all for?

In previous decades, wearing certain uniforms or carrying business cards generated respect from those around them. Whether it was a corporate suit, a pair of work boots, or a contractor's truck with a company name on the side, these symbols mattered. But what did they truly accomplish?

Many colleagues and competitors from those days are now gone. Businesses have changed hands, evolved, or simply faded away. All the branding and respect they once commanded have shifted with time. And the workers—whether in boardrooms or on loading docks, behind counters or under car hoods—are left to wonder about the lasting value of their efforts.

Yet there was always the responsibility of caring for family—real families that needed food, shelter, and education about what the world has to offer. Now those children have left the nest and are pursuing their individual ways with families of their own. The great circle of life continues.

What is the legacy when progress continues to reshape how work gets done? The Industrial Revolution transformed manufacturing and farming. Now technology is changing everything from how we conduct business to how services are delivered. The landscape keeps shifting, and each generation adapts to new tools and methods.

But perhaps this recurring cycle reveals something profound about human purpose. Each generation has watched their methods evolve, their industries transform, their certainties shift. What persisted through each change wasn't the specific work itself—it was the character forged through the commitment to do that work well.

The daily act of showing up, of caring for others despite uncertainty, of fulfilling responsibilities even when no one was watching—these choices carved something permanent into the human spirit. Parents who worked those various jobs weren't just earning paychecks; they were modeling perseverance, demonstrating that love expresses itself through dedication, teaching that dignity comes from honest work regardless of its nature or recognition.

These lessons transcend technological change. The garbage collector who takes pride in helping to keep neighborhoods clean, the small business owner who treats customers like family, the corporate manager who mentors younger employees—all are instilling the same fundamental virtues: integrity, resilience, service to others, and commitment to excellence.

These character traits become the true inheritance passed to the next generation. No matter how work evolves, those who were shaped by people of principle carry forward something invaluable: the capacity for virtue rooted in purpose. They face their own changes, their own challenges, with the same quiet dignity their predecessors demonstrated. They understand that meaning comes not from the permanence of their particular job, but from the nobility they bring to whatever work they do.

The specific businesses may change, the methods may evolve, but the souls shaped by authentic care endure. In teaching children to work with honor regardless of the task, in modeling excellence under pressure, in choosing service over selfishness—this is where the lasting legacy resides.

What was once important in terms of specific industries may shift with time. But what became important in human terms—the cultivation of character, the practice of virtue, the commitment to doing good work—these form an inheritance that transcends any particular era or technology. The circle continues not just biologically, but morally, carrying forward the nobility that makes every honest day's work meaningful, regardless of how the world around it metamorphoses.

When Autumn Comes

There is an indescribable sadness in dying. Dying, while a solitary act, invites the many connections and networks of love a person has affected prior to be a part of this final physical farewell.

Every being dies. All living things animated by the spark of life eventually will be extinguished. Those who die through some earthly tragedy or by the direct or indirect hand of others, elude the myriad of issues facing death. But for most, there is no art in dying. Most don't die gracefully or well, because the process is polluted by unceasing grasping for those last wisps of earthly life. One would think the Creator of life would have provided a better way.

Life has an unknowable expiration date, an autumn. We look back at the memories that nurtured us through the years. We summon all the childhood ones when we floated in clouds of love with our parents, grandmas and grandpas, and brothers and sisters. Then come the later memories after school was left behind, when we lived through joyful and sorrowful adventures with dear friends. Perhaps we had our own little ones, then came the day when they had their own progeny, and so on.

The question arises: Why are we here? If we are to love one another, why do so many find themselves without love? If we are here to lock arms and embrace as brothers and sisters, why do so many try to dominate their fellows? If we can't responsibly share and care for our brethren, will there be another Ark followed by a flood and renewal for the venerable ones?

Is there perhaps, as most Christians believe, a Hereafter when the Creator appears in tangible form again wielding an irresistible force of attraction that embraces the good souls with Him? At the same moment, does He release the unworthy into the abyss of oblivion?

Ruefully, autumn comes around for us all, and we weep for what once was but now is lost beyond recall. At the moment of departure, there's a profound sorrow attached to those who lived with a noble purpose; and possibly a momentary sigh of relief when the evil ones are gone.

The Journey over the Destination

Recently, I reread a poem entitled "Ithaca" by the Greek writer P.J. Cavafy. He writes about traveling to the island of Ithaca which was made famous by Homer's Odyssey. He describes the journey as something magical, something that conjures up adventures beyond the body… perhaps to the soul.

"...Hope your road is a long one,
full of adventure, full of discovery.

"...Hope your road is a long one,
May there be many summer mornings when,
with what pleasure, what joy,
you are entering harbors you are seeing for the first time;

... But don't hurry the journey at all.
Better that it lasts for years,
so you're old by the time you reach the island,
wealthy with all you gained on the way,
not expecting Ithaca to make you rich.

Ithaca gave you the marvelous journey.
Without her you wouldn't have set out.
She has nothing left to give you now.

...Wise as you will have become, so full of experience, you'll have understood by then what these Ithacas mean."

The message is the importance of the journey over the destination. We don't normally see it that way because we are always striving apart from the day at hand, looking beyond the corners to where we are headed. Perhaps we need to pause and ponder the here, here, not the there, over there.

A Glimpse into Tragedy

Those of you who read this column regularly may have noticed my enduring interest in poetry. Today I would like to share a poem that few have seen. It was written by William McHale, my grandfather, and appeared many years ago in the Chilton Times-*Journal*, which he published in the 30s and 40s.

The poem is heartfelt and sad, dealing with the death of his son in early childhood. This brings to mind the oftrepeated maxim that parents should never have to bury their children. Over the years, the poem has meant a great deal to everyone in our family, helping my siblings and cousins to remember the uncle that we lost without ever knowing him.

For Michael

Had I But Known

Had I but known he did not come to stay,
That he was just a transient little guest
By heaven sent and thither shortly bound
How avidly his smallest small request
I should have heard, and its appeasement found.

If I had known he entered at my gate
Only to pause on his far homeward flight–Sweet
soul ordained to bear no taint of earth–
How I had schemed to make the hours more bright
And shield his dimpled hands from every hurt.

But I knew not. There are tomorrows yet,
I thought, to mend the playthings wrecked today.
Then, lo, a muffling silence stilled the noise
Of clamorous mirth, for he had gone his way And
left my heart like his poor broken toys.

William McHale

The Unasked Question

There's something curious that happens in everyday conversations—at coffee shops, on planes, in waiting rooms. Someone asks how you're doing, what you do, what brings you here. You answer, maybe at length, sometimes opening up about real challenges or hopes. And then the conversation just... ends. You check your phone. They move on. The moment closes.

It's not anyone's fault. We're busy, distracted, and cautious about our limited time and energy. Talking to strangers feels like a lost art.

But here's what's easy to miss: the person asking might actually be able to help. Not in some vague, feel-good way, but concretely. Maybe they know someone hiring in your field. Maybe they've solved exactly the problem you're facing. Maybe they have access to opportunities that could genuinely matter.

The transactional cost of reciprocating is almost nothing. "What about you?" takes two seconds. But it opens a door. It creates the possibility of exchange, of discovering that the stranger making small talk might be exactly who you needed to meet.

When someone engages with you—truly engages, with genuine questions and real attention—consider engaging back. Not out of obligation, but out of curiosity. Out of recognizing that sometimes the most important connections happen in the most unexpected moments.

Because you never know who's sitting next to you.

The Elusive Quest for Eternal Youth: Reflections on the Fountain of Youth

Tales of Ponce de Leon's relentless pursuit of the mythical Fountain of Youth endure as a testament to humanity's fascination with eternal youth. Yet, as we navigate the complexities of aging, the allure of rejuvenation remains as enticing as ever.

In our quest for perpetual youth, we ponder the prospect of a second chance–a chance to relive our youth with the wisdom of age. But therein lies the paradox; for it is through the passage of time and the accumulation of experiences that we truly mature and evolve.

The notion of a reset button, tempting as it may be, raises profound questions about the essence of our existence. Are we defined by our past actions, or do we possess the capacity for reinvention? While the prospect of rewriting our life's script may seem tantalizing, it is our unique journey, with all its triumphs and tribulations, that shapes our character and molds our destiny.

As we contemplate the hypothetical existence of the Fountain of Youth, we confront the sobering reality that immortality is but a fleeting fantasy. The cyclical nature of life, with its inherent impermanence, reminds us of the preciousness of each moment and the importance of embracing the full spectrum of human experience.

Ultimately, the elusiveness of the Fountain of Youth serves as a poignant reminder that true fulfillment lies not in the pursuit of eternal youth, but in the acceptance of our mortality and the embrace of the present moment. For in the tapestry of life, it is our individual stories, woven together with threads of joy and sorrow, that imbue our existence with meaning and purpose.

Deus Ex Machina

Have you ever found yourself in a situation where everything seemed hopeless, only to have a miraculous solution present itself seemingly out of nowhere? We've all experienced these moments, where the hand of fate intervenes in our lives, providing a deus ex machina.

What, you may ask, is a deus ex machina? This Latin expression means "machine of the gods" and describes a plot device–an unexpected twist–that straightens out a situation that appeared to be irresolvable. "How did our hero escape their certain demise from that horror of horrors?" Through a deus ex machina.

From narrowly avoiding accidents to miraculously acing exams we were sure we'd fail, these instances defy rational explanation. They're the moments when the universe conspires in our favor, offering a reprieve when all seemed lost.

Deus ex machina is more than just a literary device; it's a reflection of life's mysterious ways. Sometimes, we find our own solutions through sheer determination or ingenuity. Other times, the solution finds us, appearing when we least expect it and providing a way out of situations that to all appearances were impossible.

In a world where some events defy simple explanations, deus ex machina offers a provocative frame of reference for life's inexplicable twists and turns. So, the next time you find yourself in a bind, remember that sometimes, the hand of fate is just waiting to guide you to safety. Or we might think of this as the Machinery of God working in our lives.

A Poetic Insight: Ready for Perils

In one of the timeless verses of A.E. Housman, we find a reflection and a warning of life's journey encapsulated in the poem "I to my perils".

I to my perils
    Of cheat and charmer
    Came clad in armour
By stars benign.
Hope lies to mortals
    And most believe her,
    But man deceiver
Was never mine.

The thoughts of others
    Were light and fleeting,
    Of lovers' meeting
Or luck or fame.
Mine were of trouble,
    And mine were steady;
    So I was ready
When trouble came.

These words have relevance even today, encouraging us to cultivate a sense of readiness and equip ourselves mentally and emotionally for the trials that lie ahead. Whether it be in the realm of cybersecurity, home and travel security concerns, or the myriad complexities of daily life, the principle remains the same–to be prepared, to be vigilant, and to be ready when trouble comes.

As we navigate the ever-changing currents of our world, let us embrace the ethos of readiness, recognizing that in our preparedness lies our strength, and in our resilience lies our ability to weather any storm that may come our way.

Unveiling the Echoes of Time in Shelley's "Ozymandias"

In Percy Bysshe Shelley's poignant sonnet, "Ozymandias," the reader is transported through the annals of time, encountering the echoes of voices long silenced by the sands of desert winds. Through the juxtaposition of various voices, the poem unveils the ephemeral nature of power, fame, and human existence itself.

The poem begins with a traveler's narrative, setting the scene of a vast, desolate landscape where only remnants of a once mighty civilization remain. The traveler recounts encountering a colossal statue, a monument to the arrogance and grandiosity of Ozymandias, a powerful ruler of ancient Egypt. Here, the voice of the traveler serves as a conduit, guiding the reader through the ruins of a forgotten empire.

Embedded within the traveler's narrative is the voice of the sculptor, whose artistry breathed life into the visage of Ozymandias. Through his craftsmanship, the sculptor immortalized the hubris and vanity of the ruler, capturing the essence of his reign in stone. Yet, even the most masterful of works cannot withstand the relentless march of time.

Central to the poem is the inscription on the pedestal, bearing the command of Ozymandias: "Look on my Works, ye Mighty, and despair!" This declaration, once intended to instill awe and fear in the hearts of onlookers, now serves as a bittersweet reminder of the folly of human ambition. The voice of Ozymandias himself echoes across the ages, a testament to the impermanence of power and the fleeting nature of fame.

At its core, "Ozymandias" speaks to the brevity of our existence within the vast expanse of time. Like Ozymandias and his once-great empire, we too are subject to the relentless passage of years. Our triumphs and achievements, like the shattered visage of the statue, are destined to crumble into dust, mere footnotes in the chronicles of history.

Yet, amid the ruins of empires, there is a profound beauty in the impermanence of human endeavors. It is a reminder that true greatness lies not in the accumulation of power or wealth, but in the enduring legacy of compassion, empathy, and understanding that transcends the confines of time.

In "Ozymandias," Shelley invites us to confront our own mortality and to ponder the legacy we leave behind. Through the voices of the traveler, the sculptor, and the enigmatic Ozymandias himself, we are reminded of the fragility of power, the momentary nature of fame, and the eternal march of time. It is a testament to the enduring power of poetry to capture the essence of the human experience and to illuminate the truths that bind us across the ages.

Chasing Ghosts of the Past: A Reflection

For one young woman in college, life was a vibrant tapestry, rich with suitors who embodied the epitome of earnestness. They were straight-laced, nerdy, and not conventionally handsome, yet they were kind-hearted, good people. Amidst the laughter and late-night study sessions, these suitors became a significant part of the journey, each offering a glimpse of what life could be.

However, the heart has its own compass, often pointing in unexpected directions. Despite the affection for those genuine suitors, the heart was captivated by someone different–a handsome, sweet-talking, and smart individual who stood out from the rest. This man, who would later become her husband, seemed to embody a charm and brilliance that was hard to resist.

Years rolled by, and the choice proved to be fortuitous. The once handsome, sweet-talking young man evolved into a hardworking and extremely successful husband. Together, they built a life, a family, and created a legacy through their three wonderful daughters and seven delightful grandchildren. The bonds of family grew stronger with each passing year, a testament to the love and commitment they shared.

Yet, in quiet moments, the ghosts of the past sometimes whispered to her. The what-ifs and might-have-beens lingered like shadows, making her ponder the roads not taken. The suitors of yesteryear, with their earnest eyes and kind smiles, resurfaced in memories, appearing as phantoms who might have offered a different kind of life.

But chasing these ghosts is a futile endeavor. The heart's journey, filled with its own twists and turns, led to a rich and fulfilling present. The hardworking husband, with his unwavering dedication, became the pillar of a beautiful family. His love, support, and success are real and tangible, not mere specters of possibility.

In the end, who can win at chasing the ghosts of the past? Perhaps it is not about winning but about understanding that the choices made were right for the time. The suitors of the past were part of the journey, shaping the person she became, but the path chosen led to a life filled with love, family, and legacy.

As the grandchildren's laughter fills the air and the family gathers, it becomes clear that the ghosts of the past are just that–ghosts. The present, with its richness and reality, is what truly matters. The journey of the heart is not about perfect choices but about embracing the life that has been lovingly built, one cherished moment at a time.

Ephemeral Echoes

What is the meaning of life?

I don't think the question can be answered in any universal sense. But each of us is faced with a more personal question: What is the meaning of my life?

Recently, I spent some time pondering this question and came up with some conclusions that try to answer it, at least for myself. My answer came to me in verse. If you are with me this far–the big question of meaning in life, whether short or long, whether sweet or sour–then I hope you will enjoy this poem.

In fleeting moments, our lives unfold,
A whisper of time, so brief, so bold.
We gather treasures, build empires high,
Yet dust and shadows claim them, by and by.

What worth are riches, amassed with pride,
When we depart, we leave them slide.
The houses of stone, the gold we glean,
Fade into whispers, a forgotten dream.

For in this world, our stay is brief,
A tale of joy, of pain, of grief.
We grasp at moments, clutch to hold,
Yet time slips by, relentless, cold.

We journey onward, beyond the veil,
Where earthly gains cannot prevail.
No wealth or power can cross that gate,
Only warmth and kindness we create.

So ponder not on what we own,
But on the seeds of care we've sown.
For in the end, what truly remains,
Are the hearts we've touched, the love that reigns

Let go of burdens, the worldly chase,
Embrace the light, the higher grace.
For in the end, we all must see,
There's something beyond you and me.

And as we leave, with nothing in hand,
We find our place in a promised land.
So live with purpose, love with might,
For what we leave is pure and bright.

Joy and Sorrow

The complex interplay between joy and sorrow is a timeless subject. It is perhaps not entirely fair to compare these emotions in a binary fashion. Both joy and sorrow are essential parts of the human experience–contributing to our emotional richness.

In essence, the impact of joy versus sorrow cannot be universally quantified or declared as one being greater than the other. Each emotion plays a vital role depending on an individual's circumstances and experiences. The balance of these emotions contributes to the tapestry of life, providing contrast and context that allow us to appreciate each moment more fully.

Ultimately, the significance of joy and sorrow lies in their ability to shape our lives, foster connections, and inspire personal growth. The question of which is greater may not be fair, as both are indispensable to understanding and experiencing the full spectrum of human emotion.

Embracing Stoicism

In the hustle and bustle of our modern world, it is easy to feel overwhelmed by the pressures and challenges we face daily. However, the timeless wisdom of Stoicism—as articulated by great thinkers like Seneca, Cicero, and Marcus Aurelius—offers a path to inner peace and a meaningful life. By viewing each day as a separate life, practicing restraint and moderation, regulating our emotions, and seizing the opportunities life presents, we can transform our existence.

Seneca, one of the most prominent Stoic philosophers, teaches us to live each day as if it were a complete life. This concept encourages us to focus on the present moment, appreciating the here and now without being burdened by regrets of the past or anxieties about the future. By treating each day as a new beginning, we can cultivate a sense of gratitude and purpose, making the most of our time and experiences.

Cicero, renowned for his eloquence and philosophical insights, emphasized the importance of restraint and moderation in all aspects of life. He believed that true happiness comes from balance and self-control, not from excess or indulgence. By exercising moderation in our desires and actions, we can avoid the pitfalls of overindulgence and maintain a steady course towards a virtuous and fulfilling life.

Marcus Aurelius, the Stoic emperor, provides profound guidance on regulating our emotions. In his *Meditations*, he reflects on the importance of inner tranquility and emotional resilience. By understanding that our perceptions shape our reality, we can learn to manage our responses to external events. Practicing mindfulness and self-awareness allows us to maintain our composure and clarity of thought, even in the face of adversity.

Life is fleeting, and the Stoics remind us of the urgency to seize the opportunities it offers. Seneca, Cicero, and Marcus Aurelius all highlight the importance of taking initiative and making the most of our potential. This Stoic principle encourages us to act with purpose and determination; recognizing that our time is limited and each moment is precious.

Blueprint for the End of Days

How do you want to exit this world and transition to the next?

There are two fundamental ways to approach the end of life, aside from extraordinary circumstances.

The first way is to grow old and do the ordinary things necessary to get along. You die with your hearing intact. You can still see clearly. Your voice remains strong. You have most, if not all, of your teeth, and your brain functions well enough to know what day it is. You can walk and manage basic needs independently. Ultimately, you pass away peacefully in your sleep.

The second path is to live life to the fullest, pushing your limits every day. Your vision diminishes, your voice weakens, and your hearing fades. You have only a few teeth left, and your body is marked with wrinkles and scars. You fought hard for good causes and never shied away from a challenge. You practically crawl to your grave, having given everything you had. You face the afterlife unafraid, with the remnants of your soul.

So, which path will you choose—the easy way, with its stately graces and comforts, or the challenging route, overcoming obstacles and conflicts, leaving the world a better place behind you?

The Ebb and Flow of Love

Love is one of the most profound and transformative experiences of the human condition. It can ignite our spirits, inspire our dreams, and shape our lives in ways we never imagined. But as many of us have experienced, the passionate flames of early love can dim over the years, and relationships that once felt unbreakable can face challenges and sometimes unravel. Why is it that people fall in love, only to find themselves falling out of love as time passes?

The initial spark of love often comes from a place of curiosity and excitement. It's driven by a powerful mix of physical attraction, emotional connection, and thrill of discovering someone new. In those early days, everything feels fresh and exhilarating. We see our partners through rose-colored glasses, focusing on their strengths and overlooking their flaws. This stage, often referred to as the honeymoon phase, is marked by high levels of dopamine and oxytocin, the hormones responsible for pleasure and bonding.

However, as time goes by, the intensity of these feelings naturally wanes. The routines of daily life set in, and the imperfections of our partners become more apparent. The very traits that once seemed endearing can start to feel irritating. This shift is a normal part of the relationship cycle, but it can lead to feelings of disillusionment if we don't recognize and adapt to it.

One reason people fall out of love is that they grow and change. Our experiences shape us, and as we evolve, so do our needs and desires. What brought us together initially may not sustain us as we develop new interests, values, and goals. Sometimes, couples grow together, but other times they grow apart. This divergence can create a sense of distance and incompatibility that is difficult to bridge.

Additionally, as we accumulate knowledge and experiences, our tolerance for certain behaviors can diminish. The patience we once had for minor annoyances may wear thin. The optimism that sustained us through rough patches may be replaced by a more pragmatic outlook. While this increased awareness can lead to healthier boundaries and more honest communication, it can also make us less forgiving and more critical.

Despite these challenges, falling out of love doesn't have to be the end of the story. Relationships can endure and even thrive through these transitions if both partners are willing to invest the effort. Open communication, mutual respect, and commitment to growth are essential. It's important to continually nurture the bond, finding new ways to connect and support each other.

Falling in love is often effortless, but staying in love requires intention and resilience. As we navigate the complexities of our relationships, let us remember that love is not just a feeling but a choice. It is a journey of discovery, not only of our partners, but of ourselves. Embrace the changes, cherish the memories, and strive to cultivate a love that withstands the test of time.

The Transitory Tapestry of Life

In the grand tapestry of existence, where threads of time and space weave the intricate patterns of our lives, we find ourselves often pondering the nature of our transient state. Life, as Seneca observed, is on loan to us—a fleeting gift with an inevitable expiration date. Every breath we take, every moment we cherish, is a testament to the temporality that characterizes our existence.

As we navigate through the days, we become acutely aware of the ticking clock that governs all we hold dear. Our possessions, our achievements, even our relationships, are bound by the same immutable constraints. They are all subject to the inexorable passage of time, destined to fade or transform as the sands of our personal hourglass continue to trickle down. This realization can be both humbling and enlightening, prompting us to reflect on what truly holds value in our fleeting journey.

Faith, beauty, and truth—concepts that have long captivated the human spirit—are, in fact, deeply personal constructs. Their relevance and resonance are determined by the beholder. Faith—whether in a higher power, a cause, or oneself—is a beacon that guides us through life's uncertainties. Beauty, a subjective experience, lies in the eye of the beholder, evoking emotions that range from joy to melancholy. Truth, often elusive, is a quest for meaning that varies with perspective and experience. These elements, though intangible, shape our perceptions and give color to our existence, yet they too are subject to the flow of time.

As we continue our sojourn, we must acknowledge that we are but one chapter in the ever-evolving story of humanity. Each day, new seeds of time are sown; bringing forth fresh faces, ideas, and dreams. We are continually supplanted by the next generation, each bringing their own unique contributions to the collective narrative. This cycle of renewal is a reminder of our place in the grand scheme—a single link in an endless chain of life.

The beauty of recognizing our temporal state lies in the clarity it brings. It encourages us to live with intention, to savor the fleeting moments, and to find meaning in the transient. It urges us to invest in what truly matters—our connections, our passions, and our personal growth. By embracing the impermanence of life, we can foster a deeper appreciation for the present and cultivate a legacy that, while finite, resonates beyond our own existence.

In this ephemeral dance, let us find solace and inspiration. For it is within the fleeting nature of life that we discover its true value. We are all on loan here, but in our brief tenure, we have the power to leave an indelible mark on the ever-turning pages of time.

The Saints in Our Midst

In the hustle and bustle of our daily lives, it's easy to overlook the quiet acts of kindness and the unwavering strength of character that some individuals exhibit. These rare souls, who we might call the "saints in our midst," embody virtues that transcend the ordinary. They remind us that sainthood is not a distant, unattainable ideal, but a tangible reality that can manifest in any of us, regardless of our circumstances.

We all strive for sainthood at times, in our own ways and within the limits of our capabilities. When we choose to do the right thing, despite adversity, we are tailoring ourselves to be the best versions of who we are. It's in these moments of moral clarity and strength that we brush against the essence of what it means to be saint-like. Whether it's standing up for what is right, offering a helping hand to someone in need, or simply showing love and patience in difficult situations, these acts define our potential for greatness.

Every now and then, we encounter an extraordinary person whose strength of character and capacity for love shine through. These individuals are rare, but their impact is profound. They inspire us not through grand gestures or ostentatious displays, but through their consistent, quiet commitment to virtue. In a world where money and power often dominate, they remind us that true integrity lies in the purity of our actions and intentions.

In recognizing and celebrating these saints, we also acknowledge our own potential for goodness. We may not all be destined for sainthood in the traditional sense, but we can all strive to embody the virtues that define it. By doing so, we contribute to a world that is a little kinder, a little more just, and a lot more compassionate.

"To Thine Own Self Be True"

"To thine own self be true, and it must follow, as the night the day, thou canst not then be false to any man." These words, spoken by Polonius to his son Laertes in Shakespeare's Hamlet, have echoed through the centuries, resonating with a call for authenticity and integrity. However, in today's complex and interconnected world, where societal expectations and personal aspirations often collide, living by this ancient counsel can seem both challenging and elusive.

In a society that frequently prioritizes appearances and external validation, many of us find ourselves dedicating a significant portion of our lives to meeting the perceived expectations of others. Social media platforms, professional environments, and even personal relationships can sometimes feel like stages where we perform roles designed to gain approval, admiration, or acceptance. In such a landscape, staying true to oneself can feel like a radical act of defiance.

Yet, what does it mean to be true to oneself? Is it a steadfast adherence to our core values and beliefs, regardless of external pressures? Or is it a fluid and evolving process of self-discovery and adaptation? The truth is, being true to oneself is not a one-size-fits-all proposition. Each individual's truth is unique, shaped by personal experiences, values, and aspirations. This diversity is what makes the concept both beautiful and complex.

However, a critical dilemma arises when our personal truth intersects with the truths of others. In a world filled with diverse perspectives and conflicting values, how do we navigate these intersections without losing our integrity? When our truth clashes with another's, are we compelled to compromise, or can we find a way to coexist without sacrificing our authenticity?

The reconciliation of personal truth with the expectations of others requires a delicate balance. It is not about being hypocritical but about understanding that human interactions are inherently complex. Sometimes, being true to oneself necessitates difficult conversations, empathetic listening, and a willingness to adapt without losing our essence. It means recognizing that our truth is just one part of a broader, multifaceted human experience.

As we address these intricacies, it is essential to reflect on what being true to oneself truly entails. Is it a solitary path defined solely by our perceptions and desires, or is it a journey enriched by the diverse experiences and insights of others? Perhaps the true path lies in a harmonious blend of both—an unwavering commitment to our values, coupled with an openness to learn and grow through our interactions with the world.

In conclusion, "to thine own self be true" is a timeless piece of advice that challenges us to seek authenticity in a world of constant change and varied expectations. It invites us to explore the depths of our integrity while acknowledging and respecting the diverse truths that coexist around us. As we strive to live by this principle, may we find the courage to be ourselves and the wisdom to navigate the complex interplay between personal genuineness and our shared human experience.

The True Measure of Success

In the grand tapestry of existence, we each play a fleeting role—our lives but a brief flicker in the vast expanse of time. As we age and eventually face the inevitable end, we are often compelled to ponder the true measure of success and the meaning of our existence. What purpose does our ephemeral journey serve? Why are we born to live such a brief span of life?

Traditionally, success has been quantified by wealth, status, and achievements. These tangible markers, while significant, often fail to capture the essence of a fulfilling life. True success lies not in material accumulation but in the quality of our relationships, the kindness we extend, and the impact we have on others. It is reflected in the love we give and receive, the dreams we pursue, and the resilience we exhibit in the face of adversity.

Viktor Frankl, a renowned psychiatrist and Holocaust survivor, emphasized that the search for meaning is a fundamental human drive. He argued that meaning can be found in every moment of life, even in suffering. Our purpose is not a single, grand mission but a series of small, meaningful acts that contribute to a larger whole. Whether it's through our work, our passions, or our connections with others, we create meaning daily.

Understanding that life is finite can be both daunting and liberating. It encourages us to live with intention, to cherish each moment, and to prioritize what truly matters. Our awareness of mortality can inspire us to live more fully, love more deeply, and strive to leave a positive legacy, however modest it may be. The brevity of life makes our actions more precious and our experiences more profound.

In the end, the meaning of our existence is often found in the legacy we leave behind. It's not about monumental achievements but the simple, everyday acts of kindness and the memories we create with others. Our legacy is etched in the hearts of those we touch and the positive changes we inspire. It is in the laughter shared, the wisdom imparted, and the love that endures beyond our physical presence.

The true measure of success and the meaning of life are deeply personal and often intangible. They are found in the authenticity of our journey, the depth of our connections, and the courage to live in alignment with our values. As we navigate the transient nature of our existence, let us remember that every moment holds the potential for meaning. In embracing our ephemeral nature, we discover the profound beauty of our brief, yet significant, speck of life.

Unrequited Love: A Timeless Muse in Poetry

Unrequited love has been a compelling theme in literature throughout the ages, touching the hearts of readers with its poignant and universal resonance. A long past conversation with my daughter about William Butler Yeats' poem "When You Are Old" brought this theme into sharp focus. Our discussion—enriched by insights from a University of Notre Dame professor—questioned whether Yeats' poem truly deals with unrequited love, particularly when compared to its inspiration, a French poem by Pierre de Ronsard.

Yeats, an Irish poet, penned "When You Are Old" in the late 19th century. The poem speaks to a future where the speaker's beloved, now old and gray, reflects on her past and the love she received. The lines often cited are:

> *And nodding by the fire, take down this book,*
> *And slowly read, and dream of the soft look*
> *Your eyes had once, and of their shadows deep*

The poem continues, suggesting that although many loved her beauty and grace, only one man loved her "pilgrim soul."

According to the Notre Dame professor, "When You Are Old" may not be primarily about unrequited love. Instead, it can be interpreted as a reflection on true, deep love that transcends physical beauty. The speaker laments that while others loved the beloved for her outward appearance, only he cherished her inner self. This interpretation suggests a sense of melancholy and loss, but not necessarily unrequited love.

Yeats' poem is inspired by Pierre de Ronsard's sonnet to Hélène. Ronsard's poem, "Quand vous serez bien vieille," similarly envisions a future where the beloved, now old, reflects on her past. The French poem carries a tone of regret and unrealized love, which can be seen as unrequited:

> *Quand vous serez bien vieille, au soir, à la chandelle,*
> *Assise auprès du feu, dévidant et filant,*
> *Direz, chantant mes vers, en vous émerveillant:*

Ronsard me célébrait du temps que j'étais belle.

Ronsard's lines suggest a longing for a love that was never fully reciprocated or realized, aligning more closely with the theme of unrequited love.

Is Yeats' poem about unrequited love? The answer may lie in a nuanced understanding of both poems. While Yeats' version focuses on a love that sees beyond physical beauty and feels a profound loss, it does not explicitly state that the love was unrequited. However, when seen through the lens of Ronsard's influence, we can infer a deeper layer of longing and unfulfilled desire in Yeats' work.

In the end, both interpretations hold merit. Yeats' "When You Are Old" can be seen as a reflection on true love that transcends time and beauty, while Ronsard's original poem hints more strongly at unrequited love. This duality enriches our understanding of Yeats' work, allowing readers to appreciate the complexity of love in its many forms. Unrequited love remains a timeless muse, continually inspiring poets to capture its bittersweet essence.

On Composite Selves

In the intricate tapestry of human relationships, each thread represents a unique perspective of who we are. Your mother may have seen you as a compassionate individual, always ready to lend a helping hand. Your father might have viewed you through the lens of hard work and strategic thinking, qualities that reflect his own values and aspirations for you. Your wife possibly thinks of you as a loving father, dedicated to your family and committed to nurturing your children. And in your children's eyes, you could be the dad who believes that with determination, anything is possible.

These distinct views from the people closest to us shape our identities, creating a composite of who we are. We manage our lives through the reflections of these relationships, adapting and evolving based on the roles we play. Yet, amid this dynamic interplay, it is crucial to recognize the importance of preserving a piece of our soul and heart for ourselves.

This personal reservation is not an act of selfishness but one of self-preservation. It is a sacred space where our truest selves reside, untouched and unaltered by external influences. This inner sanctum allows us to reflect, rejuvenate, and reconnect with our core values and passions. It is where our dreams take root, where our intrinsic motivations flourish, and possibly where we have the greatest impact on the lives we affect. We become better partners, parents, friends, and colleagues when we nurture our individuality. This balance enables us to give more authentically to those we love.

So, as we journey through life, let us embrace the mosaic of our composite selves. Let us cherish the diverse ways in which we are perceived and the roles we fulfill. But let us also honor the quiet, inner voice that whispers our deepest truths. In doing so, we create a harmonious blend of connection and self-awareness, enriching both our lives and the lives of those around us.

The High Cost of Estrangement

In the course of life, it's inevitable that even the closest of relationships will encounter disagreement. Whether it's a difference of opinion, a conflict of values, or something else entirely, these moments can feel incredibly significant—like hills worth dying on. But what happens when two people, bound by affection and history, find themselves at an impasse over an issue they both deem important?

At first, there's dialogue—a hope that mutual understanding will prevail. Yet, sometimes, instead of finding common ground, each party digs in deeper, their positions hardening. What follows is polarization: Both sides, convinced of their own rightness, begin to pull away from each other. Eventually, this tug-of-war leads to estrangement, where the once-close relationship is relegated to the sidelines. What was once a source of joy becomes a source of pain.

During this period of separation, each person continues to live their life. Perhaps they find new routines, new hobbies, and even new joys. But there's a profound loss here too: an unspoken void where connection once flourished. They live in separate orbits, not sharing in each other's successes, not being present in each other's challenges. On the surface, life may seem okay, even good, but there's something fundamentally missing.

Over time, as the emotional dust settles, a realization begins to dawn. What seemed like a monumental issue in the heat of the moment begins to shrink in significance. The conflict that once felt so important now seems almost trivial—a speck of dust in the grand scheme of things. And with that realization comes regret: All that time spent apart, all those moments that could have been shared, are lost forever. They missed out on the chance to support one another, to celebrate together, to simply be there for each other.

Eventually, the estrangement ends. They reconcile, recognizing the value of their relationship over the fleeting issues that drove them apart. There's relief in coming back together, in realizing that the bond between them is far more important than any disagreement. But even as they move forward, there's a lingering sense of loss for the time they wasted, the opportunities they missed to enrich each other's lives.

The truth is that life is too short for such losses. We can get tripped up by small things, but when those small things get in the way of caring for and loving one another, they're not worth the cost. When we let go of pride and stubbornness, we make space for connection and understanding. We remember that what truly matters is the relationship itself, the shared experience of life.

So, let's remind ourselves not to let the small stuff—and it's all small stuff—get in the way of the relationships that matter most. The time we have is too precious to waste on anything less.

On Aging

As we grow older, the reality of needing a little extra help to stay healthy becomes more apparent. High blood pressure, cholesterol, diabetes, asthma—these conditions often creep into our lives as we age. The truth is, once we hit 60, it's common to rely on at least one medication to manage our health. It's a fact of life, and it's not something to be ashamed of. Instead, it's a sign that we're taking the necessary steps to ensure we live longer, healthier lives.

But what can we do about this reality? First and foremost, we need to recognize that our bodies are the most precious assets we have. With just one body to carry us through life, it's essential that we take care of it—physically and mentally. That means staying active, eating well, and ensuring that our mental health is just as much of a priority as our physical health.

In the hustle and bustle of daily life, it's easy to focus only on the physical aspects of health—taking our prescribed pills, going to our doctor's appointments, monitoring our blood pressure. But mental health is equally crucial. To be dynamic, charismatic, and fully functional, we need to nurture our minds just as we do our bodies. Whether it's through meditation, social connections, hobbies, or simply taking the time to relax and de-stress, maintaining mental well-being is key to a truly healthy life.

So, while it's true that pills may become a necessary part of our daily routine, let's not forget that they're just one tool in our arsenal. A healthy lifestyle—both physically and mentally—can make all the difference in how we age and how we feel. Let's embrace the fact that, with the right support, we can live vibrant, fulfilling lives, no matter what age we are.

Reaching Beyond the Veil

In the quiet moments of reflection, when the world around us falls still, it is natural to wonder about those who have gone before us. They lived, they loved, they achieved noble purposes, and now, they dwell in the spiritual realm—a world that seems distant yet so intimately connected to our own. The question arises: can we summon their guidance, their wisdom, to help us navigate the challenges of life and fulfill our own noble purposes?

It is a comforting thought to imagine that those we cherished in life could reach back across the divide to offer us support. We often think of them as watching over us; their presence felt in the whispers of intuition or the sudden, inexplicable clarity that descends upon us in moments of need. But is there a way to actively seek their counsel, to draw upon their strengths and love in a way that influences our own journey?

The idea of summoning those who have passed, much like Aladdin's three wishes, is a compelling one. Yet, unlike a magical lamp, the spiritual world operates on principles that we may not fully comprehend. Perhaps it is not a matter of summoning, but rather of aligning ourselves with the higher purposes they embodied. When our goals are steeped in goodness and love, when we strive to add light to a world often shrouded in darkness, we may find that their influence naturally flows into our lives. It is as though the veil between the physical and spiritual world thins, allowing their energy to blend with ours.

This raises the question: Are we truly alone in our struggles, left to our own devices to fight dragons and defend the vulnerable? Or are we, in fact, accompanied by unseen forces—guardian angels assigned to us in childhood, perhaps, or angelic warrior guides who step in as we mature? These beings, if they exist, could be seen as extensions of the love and guidance from those who have departed. They are the guardians of our souls, nudging us toward the right path, helping us bear the burdens that life inevitably places upon us.

As hybrids of the physical and spiritual realms, we walk a unique path. Our souls, tethered to this world by the body, are still deeply connected to the spiritual plane. In our imperfection, we long for the perfection that our souls might achieve once freed from the body. But what if we could draw upon that spiritual perfection even now? What if we could channel some of the purity and wisdom from the other side into our daily lives?

It is possible, perhaps, to reach out and connect with the spiritual world more intentionally. Through prayer, meditation, or simply living a life aligned with higher principles, we might open ourselves to the influence of those who have gone before us. In doing so, we are not only connecting with them but also drawing from the eternal into the finite. We become conduits for the love and wisdom that transcends this earthly existence, allowing it to flow through us and into the world around us.

Ultimately, life may indeed be a test, a proving ground for the soul. But it is also an opportunity—a chance to blend the physical with the spiritual, to draw upon the resources of both worlds as we strive to fulfill our purpose. And in this endeavor, we are not alone. The spiritual world, with all its love and wisdom, is closer than we think, ready to support us as we walk our path.

So, as we move forward, let us do so with the knowledge that we are supported by those who have gone before us, by guardian angels, and by the very perfection that awaits us in the spiritual realm. We are here for a reason, and with the help of the unseen, we can fulfill that purpose with grace and courage.

Celebrating the Visionaries Among Us

In every community, there are those special individuals who live on the edge of brilliance, straddling the fine line between genius and madness. They are the dreamers, the visionaries, the ones who see beyond the horizon, imagining possibilities that most of us could never conceive. These remarkable people often go unrecognized and misunderstood, yet their contributions shape our world in ways that are profound and lasting.

These trailblazers have accomplished so much for the good of the world, though their work is often ahead of its time. They pioneer new frontiers, breaking down the traditional barriers that confine our thinking and stifle innovation. In doing so, they create spaces that the world never even imagined before they were born. Their work is not just about advancing technology, science, or art—it's about expanding the very limits of what it means to be human.

In our community, we are fortunate to have such individuals among us. They are not always easy to understand, nor do they have to be. Their ideas may seem outlandish, their methods unconventional, and their perspectives radical, but it is precisely this that makes them so valuable. They challenge us to think differently, to question the status quo, and to embrace change, even when it is uncomfortable.

These are the people who remind us that progress is not about playing it safe. It's about daring to venture into the unknown, to take risks, and to push the boundaries of what is possible. They are the catalysts for transformation, the ones who inspire us to dream bigger and reach further.

As we move forward as a community, let us take a moment to recognize and appreciate these unique individuals. They are the sparks that ignite the flames of innovation and progress. And while their brilliance may not always be immediately understood, their legacy will be felt for generations to come.

Let us celebrate the visionaries among us, for they are the pioneers of tomorrow, lighting the way to a future that is brighter, bolder, and more beautiful than we could ever imagine.

The Power of a Name

In a world filled with words, there is one that stands out above all others—a word that is the most cherished, the most appealing, and the most significant to each of us. That word is our own name.

Whether your name is Mary, Anne, Steve, or Brian, there is an undeniable truth: hearing your name spoken by someone else is a powerful experience. It resonates in a way that no other word can, because it is tied to your identity, your existence, and your place in the world.

Names are unique, yet they are also common. They might be shared by thousands, but when it is your name, it feels singular, special, and deeply personal. It is a word that signifies who you are, and when others remember and use it, it signifies that you are seen, recognized, and valued.

That is why, when you meet someone new and they tell you their name, the best thing you can do is to remember it. And not just remember it—use it. The next time you see that person, whether it's days, weeks, or even months later, addressing them by name is a small but profound gesture. It tells them that you cared enough to remember, that they left an impression on you, and that you appreciate who they are as an individual.

In a broader sense, remembering and using someone's name is about more than just social etiquette. It's about building connections, fostering relationships, and influencing others in a positive way. When we acknowledge someone by name, we are not just recognizing their presence; we are affirming their worth.

So, as we go through life, meeting new people and forming new connections, let's remember the power of a name. It's the starting point of understanding others. And in a world where everyone wants to be seen and heard, sometimes all it takes is remembering one simple word—their name.

Becoming Instruments of God's Peace

As we go through life, there's one undeniable truth we all share: we are all going to die. This sobering reality has been with us since the dawn of humanity, yet we often fail to confront it until we're forced to. But what if, instead of avoiding this truth, we embraced it as a powerful motivator? What if we used it to drive us toward something greater than ourselves?

Imagine if, knowing that our time here is limited, we dedicated our lives to becoming instruments of God's peace. Imagine if we became peacemakers in a world that so desperately needs peace. The concept isn't new—it's been the call of countless prophets, leaders, and thinkers throughout history. But now, perhaps more than ever, it's a call we need to answer.

Why don't we? Why don't we choose to be God's peacemakers, to show kindness and love that extends beyond our own material needs and desires? Perhaps it's fear, or perhaps it's because we're so often caught up in the mundane routines of life. We focus on accumulating wealth, power, and possessions, thinking that these things will bring us happiness. But deep down, we know that they won't. True fulfillment comes from something far more profound.

What if God's plan all along has been for us to figure out that we're here to spread peace and love? What if our highest calling is to reach out to others, to transcend our own selfish needs, and to show acts of kindness and compassion? It's a simple idea, yet it's incredibly powerful.

Think about the impact we could have if each of us made the conscious decision to be a peacemaker. If we chose to resolve conflicts rather than create them, to build bridges rather than walls, to spread love rather than hate. The ripple effect of our actions could transform not just our immediate circles, but the world at large.

As instruments of God's peace, we have the opportunity to leave a lasting legacy. We can make a difference in a world that often seems lost in chaos and division. And in doing so, we can find a sense of purpose that goes far beyond our individual lives.

So, let us ask ourselves: why not? Why not become peacemakers? Why not live our lives in a way that reflects the love and kindness that God has shown us? Why not strive to leave the world a better place than we found it?

In the end, we all will face the same fate. But until that day comes, let's commit to living our lives as instruments of peace. Let's reach beyond our material needs, show love to those around us, and embrace the calling that has been with us all along. We may just find that in doing so, we fulfill the very purpose of our existence.

Not Them. Us.

I want you to think back to a moment in your life when you felt fear about money. Perhaps you were laid off and watched your savings dwindle. Maybe a medical emergency emptied your bank account. Or you remember your parents whispering anxiously at the kitchen table, trying to figure out which bill to pay first.

That knot in your stomach—that's where homelessness begins.

For most of us, something intervened. Family helped. A new job came through. Insurance covered enough. We stepped back from the edge. But for thousands of our Wisconsin neighbors, that safety net never appeared, or it tore under the weight of circumstances no one should have to bear alone.

Homelessness doesn't always look like what we imagine. It's the family sleeping in their car in a Walmart parking lot because Dad's hours got cut. It's the veteran whose PTSD makes it impossible to hold down steady work. It's the single mother choosing between rent and her daughter's medication. It's the young person who aged out of foster care with nowhere to go. It's the mental health crisis that spiraled without access to treatment. The medical bill that became a mountain. The domestic violence survivor who fled with nothing but her children and her life.

Any one of these stories could have been ours. The distance between housed and homeless is often just one catastrophe, one missed paycheck, one moment when everything falls apart at once.

On October 10, we observe Homelessness Awareness Day—not to feel good about our awareness, but to commit to action. Our state campaign has launched with facts, figures, and resources on how to help. But before I ask you to act, I want you to understand why it matters. We live in Wisconsin—a state blessed with more than enough. We live in a country overflowing with bounty. The question isn't whether we have the resources to address homelessness. The question is whether we have the will.

Those who have more than they need should share with those who do not. This isn't charity; it's community. It's recognizing that our neighbor's suffering diminishes us all, and their dignity restored elevates everyone.

Volunteer your time. Shelters, food banks, and outreach programs need hands and hearts. An hour of your week could mean everything to someone rebuilding their life. Donate what you can. Whether it's money, warm clothing, or hygiene supplies, your contribution matters. No gift is too small when it comes from genuine care.

And perhaps most importantly, extend compassion. When you see someone experiencing homelessness, remember: you don't know their story. You don't know what they've survived. Meet them with the same humanity you'd want if you were in their place.

The path to ending homelessness isn't mysterious. It requires affordable housing, accessible mental health care, living wages, and a commitment to treating every person with dignity. It requires all of us deciding that no one should sleep outside in a Wisconsin winter. No child should go to school wondering where they'll sleep that night.

Our statewide campaign provides concrete ways to get involved. But beyond any specific program, I'm asking you to make a personal commitment. Find one way—just one—to make a difference. Volunteer when you can. Make a donation. Advocate for policies that address root causes. Talk to your children about compassion without condescension.

Homelessness doesn't have to be permanent. Together, we can work to ameliorate this crisis—and someday, yes, extinguish it entirely. But only if we choose to see, to care, and to act.

Finding the Perfect Someone

Life's treasures aren't measured in material possessions like a sleek car or a spacious mansion. You could have all of these things, but without someone to share them with, what do they really mean? Isn't life truly about finding that perfect someone—a person who turns the ordinary into extraordinary?

We long for someone who is more than just a partner; someone who is witty, who lights up the room with a smile, and who can turn even the dullest moments into something unforgettable. This is the person who finishes your sentences, who has your back without question, who loves you with a fierce loyalty that never wavers.

Together, you become more than just individuals; you are a team, a unit that others see as one. Friends and family expect to see you together, and even children instinctively ask for the other when only one is present.

But what happens when that magical connection is suddenly severed? How do you navigate life without the person who brought joy to your every day, who was your constant in a world full of change? How do you move forward knowing that no one will ever quite match what they brought to your life?

Finding the perfect person means everything. It's a rare and beautiful gift that, once lost, leaves a void nothing else can fill.

We Are One

I am not just one; I am a unit of many—my ancestors who paved the way, the stages of my life shaped by community and friends, and the family of God's creation to which we all belong.

Whatever I do is not just me; it is many. We are all in this together. No one deserves all the credit, and no one should bear all the blame. Our successes and failures are collective, reflecting the journey we share.

So, let's make it worthwhile. Let's journey together with love and compassion, setting aside denigration and hate. Our shared path is our greatest responsibility and our most profound opportunity.

The Gift of Life and The Inevitable Abyss

One of God's greatest gifts is the gift of life. But that gift comes with an expiration date. In the grand scheme of eternity, our time on this earth is just a speck—here today, gone tomorrow. No matter who we are, where we come from, or what we accomplish, the end awaits us all. And when our time runs out, we disappear into the abyss of humanity, fading away into the vast ocean of those who have come before us.

We all leave our mark—some big, some small. Some build empires that echo through the ages, while others quietly tend to their families, neighborhoods, or communities. No matter the scale, each mark has value. But eventually, every empire crumbles, every accomplishment is forgotten, and every individual falls into the same great oblivion. It's a humbling reality and a universal truth.

So, knowing this, the question remains: What do you want to do with your life?

Will you spend your days chasing material things that rust and decay, or will you invest in moments that last beyond your time here—moments of kindness, love, and connection that ripple through the lives of others? Will you lift up those around you, plant seeds of goodness, and be an instrument of peace, or will you let your days slip away, consumed by the trivial?

Life is fleeting, and none of us know how much time we have. But within this brief window, we all have a choice. What legacy will you leave? What will you do with your gift of life? Will you simply exist, or will you dare to make your mark?

Our moments are few, and our time is short. But even a small spark can light up the darkness. So, let's make it count. Before we vanish into the abyss, let us live with purpose, gratitude, and a commitment to make the world just a little bit better for those who will follow.

The Games We Play: Time-Wasters or Strategic Tools

When I was young, gaming meant dropping a coin into a pinball machine or, later on, playing Pac-Man and Pong. These simple games were a far cry from today's complex digital worlds. Now, on flights or in waiting rooms, I see people glued to their screens, playing Word Solitaire and other mind teasers. Many think these games keep their minds sharp, staving off dementia in later years. But I can't help but wonder: Are these games more than unproductive time-wasters?

My grandsons are drawn to more intense digital realms, where they engage in city brawls and battle against endless waves of bad guys. They win some, lose some, and, more often than not, find themselves strategizing their next attack to live another round. It's easy to dismiss these games as frivolous or even harmful. After all, they occupy hours that could be spent outdoors, reading, or building something tangible. But maybe there's more to the story.

Could it be that these games are sharpening their minds, fostering strategic thinking, and teaching them to navigate complex challenges? Or are they merely addictions, designed to keep them tethered to screens at the expense of real-world experiences and deeper purpose?

It's a question worth asking: Are we losing valuable time, or are we, in some odd way, training ourselves for a world that increasingly values quick thinking, adaptability, and, yes, a warrior-like mentality? Are these games shaping our lives in meaningful ways, or are they just another form of distraction in a world already overflowing with them?

In the end, perhaps the bigger question isn't just about the games but about what we value in life. Do we want to cultivate real skills, real connections, and real experiences, or are we content with virtual victories that fade as soon as we put down the controller?

The Human Condition and Its Many Variations

Remember the song "Just Dropped In (To See What Condition My Condition Was In)" by Kenny Rogers and the First Edition? In today's world, rare indeed is the person who enjoys what we might call perfect health. It seems that nearly everyone is managing some condition—whether it's asthma, high blood pressure, cholesterol issues, diabetes, heart disease, or one of countless other ailments. The human condition itself appears fraught with conditions, ranging from the mild to the severe.

We try our best—eating well, exercising, following doctors' orders—but even with all our efforts, good health isn't guaranteed. It can be elusive, slipping through our fingers no matter how tightly we try to hold on. And so, we adapt. We manage. We roll with the flow, accepting that our bodies, like our lives, are imperfect.

Perhaps it's this imperfection that makes the human experience all the more poignant. Life is never entirely smooth, nor is health, but we endure and continue on, adjusting as we go. In a way, the conditions we face are just part of the larger condition we all share: being human.

The Better Half

In the first half of life, many people are driven by a desire for achievement, status, and wealth. Their energy is focused outward, fueled by ambition, competition, and the pursuit of tangible rewards. They define success in terms of material gain and recognition from others—feeding the body and self-image, often in a restless quest for more. Their essence becomes intertwined with the identity they construct through aggressive actions and societal expectations.

But as they enter the second half of life, the tide shifts. The outer world, with its demands for money and power, loses its grip. These individuals have achieved much—perhaps too much—and now they begin to hear the quieter call of the soul. It's a transition from external striving to internal reflection, a shift from "doing" to "being."

In this phase, the emphasis on material things, titles, and accolades fades. They realize that no matter how much they accumulate, it can never fully satisfy the deeper hunger for meaning and fulfillment. So, they turn inward, seeking to nourish the soul instead of the body, shifting their focus to things of lasting value—relationships, legacy, inner peace, and wisdom.

Like travelers who have returned from an epic journey, they no longer feel the same urge to conquer new territories. Instead, they are content to "be" in the moment, to observe, and to reflect rather than to push and assert. They are less concerned with leaving a mark on the world, for they have come to understand that true contentment lies not in the chase but in the arrival.

They may still seek adventure, but it's a different kind—one that nurtures the soul rather than the ego. This phase of life is not about acquiring more, but about letting go, about finding peace in simplicity and embracing the richness of the present moment. The second half of life is about becoming whole, about uniting the outward success with inner serenity. They are no longer climbing the mountain; they are sitting on the summit, taking in the view.

Grave Thoughts From the Graveyard

Today, I visited a graveyard to pay my respects to a recently departed family member. The cemetery was vast, and we found ourselves lost amid rows of unfamiliar headstones. After wandering both on foot and by car, weaving past names unknown to us, we finally reached the gravesite.

Standing there, I couldn't help but think about this place—where those who were once so visible and vibrant in life are laid to rest, becoming part of the quiet, unremembered landscape. The sun beat down with hardly any shade, and the graves seemed tightly packed, which made me wonder about the business side of burial plots—how every inch is planned, sold, and filled.

But more than that, my mind wandered to the fate of the souls. After death, where do they go? Surely, they don't linger here. While the dead no longer have a care or say in their resting place, there's an undeniable finality to it. They are gone from the world we know; and at an immediate or lingering point in time, their bodies become the forgotten invisible. After all of their toils, they are buried away somewhere out of sight, and out of mind.

Reconciling the Existence of God with the Concept of Faith

In the Christian worldview, the existence of God and the nature of faith are intricately linked but not necessarily in tension. Christianity holds that God has revealed Himself in both general revelation (the natural world and human reason) and special revelation (the Bible and the person of Jesus Christ). So, Christians believe that God's existence can be rationally demonstrated to a certain degree through philosophical arguments, scientific evidence, and human experience.

However, Christianity also teaches that humanity's finite understanding means we cannot fully comprehend the infinite God through reason alone. This is where faith comes in—it is the way by which we trust in and apprehend spiritual realities that transcend human reason. Faith does not negate reason but rather complements it and allows us to access a deeper, more holistic knowledge of God.

Reconciling faith and reason is an age-old challenge in Christian thought, but most Christian theologians would say they are not mutually exclusive. The Christian life involves both a rational consideration of the evidence for God's existence and a personal trust, commitment, and relationship with this God. In this view, reason can lead one to the possibility of God's existence, but faith is required to truly know and relate to Him.

Ultimately, Christianity teaches that faith and reason work together—faith informs and enriches our rational understanding, while reason helps strengthen and give coherence to our faith. The goal is not to pit them against each other, but to see them as complementary pathways to knowing the God Christians believe has made Himself known.

The Body Electric: Our Brief Dance on Earth

We shape these vessels we inhabit in myriad ways. Some forge their bodies into instruments of physical mastery—swimmers cutting through water with precision, quarterbacks reading the field in split seconds, squash players dancing across courts with balletic grace. Years of dedication might lead to an Olympic podium or professional glory, though few reach those rarefied heights.

Then there are those who cultivate the mind within the body's framework. They delve into engineering's complexities, unravel accounting's precision, or navigate the law's labyrinthine paths. Their muscles may not ripple, but their intellects illuminate the darkness of human ignorance.

A third tribe exists: the creators, the dreamers. Their hands shape clay, their voices weave melodies, their words paint worlds unseen. They pluck at the strings of human consciousness, composing symphonies of experience that resonate through time.

Each group finds its purpose—a way to declare "I was here" or carve their names into the bark of existence. But a deeper question lurks beneath these pursuits: Is this all there is? We develop our gifts, chase excellence, and gather accolades—yet for what? Are these achievements merely footnotes in the vast book of time?

Is this earthly playground—with its medals, degrees, and masterpieces—truly what some divine architect intended? Or are we missing something profound as we scramble to excel in our chosen arenas? Have we mistaken the accumulation of achievements—whether physical, intellectual, or creative—for genuine purpose?

We've built civilizations, created systems to distribute resources, established hierarchies of control—all within the briefest flicker of cosmic time. Each of us operates within these structures, striving and competing, until age or fate draws the final curtain.

The question echoes: What are we really doing here? Why are we granted these finite moments, these precious slivers of consciousness, only to have them slip away like sand through our fingers? Perhaps the answer lies not in what we achieve, but in how we spend these fleeting moments—and whether we dare to question their meaning at all.

Autumn Leaves

We are all like paper dolls, adorning ourselves in the world's trinkets and trappings. We parade through life draped in materials that mask our true essence—designer labels, status symbols, carefully curated personas. Yet strip away these earthly decorations, and what remains? Our eternal souls, pure and unadorned, preparing for their journey beyond this material masquerade.

For all our worldly costumes and social performances, we are merely spiritual beings passing through a temporary stage. At day's end, we shed these material shells like autumn leaves, revealing the luminous truth of who we really are—souls destined for realms where earthly facades hold no meaning, where only our spiritual essence endures.

Integrating the Shadows and Ghosts

The past has a peculiar way of walking beside us, especially when it takes the shape of someone we've lost. You carry her in fragments—perhaps the echo of her high octave laugh, the way she'd tilt her head when listening, or how she'd wrestle on an innocent childhood blanket of grass. These aren't just memories; they're imprints that have become part of your emotional architecture.

But here's the complexity: this person who shaped part of your childhood continues to cast a shadow over your present, unaware of her posthumous influence. She exists in a kind of double exposure—the person she was then, frozen in time, and the ghost she's become in your evolving narrative. Each recollection is both a comfort and a reminder of absence, like pressing on a bruise to remember its tenderness.

The challenge isn't about letting go; it's about learning to interlace this sometime-memory into the mosaic of your present life without letting it overshadow the colors of your ongoing story.

Human Body Design

When we stop to think about the design of the human body, we might find ourselves wondering if it could have been crafted more efficiently. Consider the everyday processes of hydration and nutrition: why must we spend so much of our lives urinating or expelling waste from our bodies? Couldn't we have been designed to hydrate through the skin, or metabolize food directly into energy without the need for waste?

It's a curious thought experiment—imagining a body that functions without the need to "offload" its excesses, freeing us from the sometimes-inconvenient realities of biological maintenance. Wouldn't it be wonderful to live unencumbered by these daily rituals, focusing solely on the higher pursuits of life?

Yet, when we reflect more deeply, we realize that the human body as it is designed is nothing short of miraculous. It's a complex, harmonious system where countless processes—digestion, circulation, respiration—work in synchrony to sustain us. These so-called inefficiencies might actually be part of the greater design, teaching us humility and grounding us in the rhythms of life. They remind us of our interconnectedness with nature and the delicate balance we inhabit.

Could there have been a "better" design? Perhaps. But then, would we be the same creatures we are now—resilient, adaptable, and marvelously imperfect? Perhaps the true genius of the human design lies not in its flawlessness, but in its resilience and ability to grow through imperfection.

What Is Truly Important in Life?

We often find ourselves captivated by the extraordinary—running with the bulls in Pamplona, climbing ancient mountains in Peru, or riding the storied trains of Europe. These adventures are thrilling, vivid brushstrokes on the canvas of life. Yet, they are only moments, flashes in time. Life's true essence often lies in the subtler, quieter moments: the joy of a shared laugh, the warmth of a tender embrace, the lessons learned from arguments and reconciliation with those we hold dear.

A life lived with purpose is often shaped by love—a love that grounds us, challenges us, and inspires us to grow. From this love, legacies are born: Children who carry your values into the world, extended family who share in their journey, and grandchildren who magically embody hope and promise. It is in these relationships, nurtured and cherished, that the importance of life becomes clear.

So, what is of importance? It is not just the grand adventures but the bonds we create, the kindness we extend, and the wisdom we pass down. It's about living in a way that resonates beyond our own time, leaving behind a legacy of love, integrity, and meaningful connection.

The brevity of life demands that we ask hard questions: How do we spend our fleeting years? What will we leave behind? The answer lies not in material achievements but in the impact we have on others and the moments of joy, love, and peace we cultivate.

Life's importance is found in being present, in building something greater than ourselves, and in ensuring that, even as we are but a speck on this vast planet, our lives have left a meaningful imprint on the hearts of those we love.

The Implications of Telling a Lie

Let's consider what it means when someone tells a lie. Whether it's told to one person or many—depending on the liar's available platforms—the essence remains the same: they knowingly state something untrue. They don't believe it themselves because they know it's false. Yet, they say it anyway.

What are the implications of knowingly spreading falsehoods?

Does it reflect on the person's integrity and diminish our ability to trust them in the future? Trust is often hard-earned and easily lost. If someone repeatedly speaks falsehoods, does it reveal something about their character—about who they truly are?

And what happens when the lies multiply? What if the person telling them holds a position of authority or influence? Do their lies carry more weight, affecting not just individual relationships but entire communities or societies?

As a society, we often wrestle with how to respond to liars. Do we simply tolerate them, resigning ourselves to the noise of their falsehoods? Or do we take a stand—choosing to distance ourselves, challenge their statements, or even remove them from our lives altogether?

The act of lying is never a neutral one. It leaves a mark, not only on the deceived but also on the deceiver. It erodes trust, fractures relationships, and undermines the fabric of any community. Yet, each of us has a choice in how we respond: to confront lies with truth, to rebuild trust where it has been broken, or to protect ourselves by stepping away.

Protected Moments in Time: A Reflection on Love and Change

In life, we all experience what I'd call "protected moments in time"—those rare and powerful instances where everything feels eternal. Perhaps it was the day you fell in love and promised a "forever" to someone, or a lifechanging experience where a vow to stay true felt as solid as the stars. In these moments, we see our highest ideals, our best selves, and we genuinely believe that nothing will shake that promise.

Yet, life has a way of unfolding unpredictably. Years pass, circumstances change, and sometimes, so do we. We might find ourselves looking back at those once-immovable promises, wondering if they are still meant to shape our lives now. It's a complex question: Do we remain loyal to the person we once were, honoring that promise? Or do we let that moment live as a cherished memory, appreciating it for what it was, even if we have outgrown it?

As we grow, perhaps part of honoring these protected moments is acknowledging that they held real meaning and value, even if time has carried us in different directions. It's about asking ourselves how these moments can be preserved—not necessarily as obligations but as threads in the fabric of our lives. In this way, those precious promises don't have to be lost or broken; instead, they become a part of who we are today, even as we embrace the person we've become.

Opening this dialogue invites us to look at our lives with compassion, respect, and honesty. It allows us to honor our past without being held captive by it, and perhaps to understand that some promises were meant to live beautifully in memory, influencing us, but not confining us. In these reflections, we might find peace, and maybe even inspiration, to continue building moments worth protecting in the time we have.

Looking Past; Looking Forward

When the love of your life dies, the impact is profound and life-altering. The grief can feel as though it will never subside, and the absence of that person—your partner in all things—casts a shadow over even the smallest moments of your day. The process of losing them, from illness or sudden tragedy to the final goodbye, is one of life's greatest challenges.

After the funeral is over, the loneliness often sets in deeply. Friends and family may surround you for a time, offering kindness and support, but eventually, their lives pull them back to their routines. And there you are, left to grapple with the silence.

Many who experience such a loss have shared how the grief feels inescapable. The routines and memories you shared with your spouse linger everywhere—in your home, your daily habits, and even in the way you think about the world. The ache is particularly acute when something good or bad happens, and you instinctively want to share it with them.

There is no one-size-fits-all answer to coping with such loss. Each person's grief is unique, shaped by the depth of the relationship and the individual personality of the one left behind. However, here are some thoughts that may offer comfort and guidance as you navigate this painful journey.

First, take it one day at a time. It's simple advice, but it holds profound wisdom. In the early days, just getting out of bed and facing the world can feel like a monumental task. Allow yourself to move at your own pace. Don't rush the grieving process or feel pressured to "move on" too quickly. Healing is not linear, and it's okay to have days when the sorrow feels overwhelming.

It's important to lean on others—but also seek to rebuild. Family and friends can provide crucial support, but their lives will naturally continue. You may find yourself needing to rebuild parts of your own. Consider joining a grief support group where others who've experienced similar losses can share their insights and struggles. Knowing you're not alone in your feelings can be deeply reassuring.

Over time, you can find new meaning and purpose. Though it feels impossible at first, try to slowly re-engage with the world. Take up an activity or explore something you've always been curious about. Join a class in art, writing, or history. Volunteer with an organization that aligns with your values. If you're physically able, activities like yoga, gardening, or walking in nature can offer both physical and emotional relief.

You may find some healing in honoring your loved one's memory. Create a ritual or space where you can remember and celebrate your spouse. It might be a small garden, a photo album, or even a weekly moment of reflection. This helps keep them present in your life in a way that feels healthy and comforting, rather than overwhelming.

But don't remain in a constant state of sorrow. Your loved one wouldn't want that. While they may no longer be physically by your side, their love and influence live on in you. Embracing life doesn't mean forgetting them; it means carrying their memory with you as you find joy again.

Take heart, dear reader. Though the journey of loss is painful, it's also a testament to the love you shared. Grief is a long and winding road, but it does not mean your own story is over. It's a new chapter—one you didn't ask for, but one in which you can still find meaning, connection, and even hope.

Little Bursts of Happiness

In a world bustling with deadlines, distractions, and the unrelenting hum of routine, it's easy to overlook the extraordinary in the ordinary. Yet, it's in those fleeting moments—at the checkout line, on a flight, or in a quick business transaction—where we hold the power to create something profound: a little burst of happiness.

It doesn't take much. A smile, a kind word, or a genuine question like, "How's your day going?" can transform an interaction from transactional to meaningful. Sometimes, though, a small token—a physical reminder of goodwill—can spark a ripple effect of positivity. My favorite? A $2 bill.

The $2 bill is iconic, rare enough to feel special but common enough to be accessible. Handing it to someone with a simple message—"This is for luck, and I hope it brings you good fortune"—does more than exchange paper. It says, I see you. You matter. I've passed them to retail clerks who look weary from hours of scanning barcodes, to pilots who ensure our safe passage through the skies, and to business associates who are navigating the grind. The reactions vary—some are puzzled, others light up with surprise—but almost always, there's a smile.

What happens next is where the magic begins. That $2 bill becomes a conversation starter, a keepsake, or maybe even a nudge toward dreaming bigger. It's not about the monetary value; it's about the gesture, the reminder that hope and good fortune are still within reach. The beauty of these small acts is how they inspire us to try harder, be better, and dream more. They remind us that life, for all its unpredictability, holds space for kindness. And perhaps, with enough of these little bursts of happiness, we can create a world where the ordinary feels extraordinary.

So, the next time you find yourself face-to-face with someone in the course of your day, take a moment. Pass along a smile, a kind word, or even a $2 bill. You never know how far that spark of hope might travel—or how brightly it might shine.

Intersections, Engagements, and Disruptions

Life is full of intersections—moments where paths cross, perspectives meet, and opportunities arise to create something greater than ourselves. At these intersections, we find engagements—a call to connect, to listen, and to act. And often, there's disruption—a shake-up of our usual rhythm that challenges us to respond with courage and creativity. But how often do we miss these moments? How often do we keep our heads down, too distracted or too hurried to notice the person in need, the injustice unfolding, or the chance to bring light into someone's darkness?

To truly make a difference, we must learn to engage with life at these intersections. This requires us to pay attention—to be fully present in our surroundings and aware of what's unfolding around us. It requires us to listen—to hear not only what is spoken but also what is unsaid. And it requires us to move—to step into the role of difference-maker, sometimes in ways that feel almost heroic.

The truth is, we don't need capes or superpowers to change the world. Small, deliberate actions have the power to create ripples far beyond what we can imagine. A word of encouragement can rebuild someone's confidence. A helping hand can restore hope. An act of kindness can spark a chain reaction of good. Yet, in a world that often feels fragmented, it's easy to hesitate. We wonder if we're qualified, if our efforts matter, or if we'll be misunderstood. But isn't it better to risk doing good than to remain on the sidelines, wondering what could have been?

Imagine a world where each of us stepped into these moments with boldness—where we treat every intersection as sacred, every engagement as an opportunity, and every disruption as a call to action. Imagine the change we could inspire, the lives we could uplift, and the hope we could ignite. Life's intersections are not random; they are invitations. Will you accept?

Wish I Was an Angel

Sometimes I wish I was an angel—able to do all good things, bring out the best in people, and lift their spirits. Imagine waking each day with a single purpose: to help, to heal, to inspire. Angels, in their divine simplicity, seem to exist for no other reason than to spread light and love. But perhaps being an angel isn't so far out of reach for any of us. What if we looked at our own lives and asked how we might bring a little more kindness into the world? Couldn't we all be angels on earth in some small way?

It doesn't take much. A smile shared with a stranger, a listening ear for someone struggling, a word of encouragement when someone falters. Sometimes, it's just showing up when someone needs you—no fanfare, no grand gestures. These simple acts of compassion can remind others of their worth and potential, gently nudging them toward their better selves.

We've all met someone who, for a fleeting moment, made us feel like life wasn't so heavy. A teacher, a neighbor, a friend, or even a stranger who held the door with a kind word or saw something in us we hadn't seen in ourselves. Those people are the angels among us, and we can be that for someone else too.

So, let's make today wonderful—not by chasing perfection but by spreading a little hope, lending a helping hand, or simply being present. In these small, quiet ways, we can bring heaven a little closer to earth. Who knows? Maybe that's what angels really are—the best versions of us, shining through.

The Inside In or the Outside Out

When I was young, love seemed like something you could measure in glances. I wanted a pretty girl—the kind that turned heads and made other guys envious. I'd walk into a room with her, and the looks we'd get felt like a raised eyebrow and a quiet "Wow, buddy, how'd you do that?" In my mind, I'd say to everyone watching, "Eat your hearts out."

How shallow that seems now.

Time has a way of showing you what really matters. It took years—and some heartbreaks—for me to realize that beauty on the outside pales next to the beauty within. Now, as I look back, I treasure the richness of the life I share with someone who knows me at my core. She is not just my partner but my most trusted friend, the keeper of my past, and the compass for my future. She embodies the familiarity of family, the comfort of shared memories, and the strength of shared virtues.

I almost missed it. I was so busy casting for the surface that I nearly overlooked the depth. But by some miracle of fate—or grace—my last cast in the pool connected me to the love I didn't even know I needed.

Now, I wake up each day beside her, and the morning sun shines a little brighter. The stars twinkle a little more at night. She makes the world go round. Not with the kind of beauty that fades but with the kind that grows richer, deeper, and more radiant with every passing year.

To anyone still searching or holding out for the "wow" factor, I say this: Look deeper. True beauty isn't something you show off to the world; it's something that wraps itself around your heart, fills your soul, and makes life worth living.

On Aging and Invisibility

As we age, we begin to relinquish the power and foundation we spent a lifetime building. The network of friends, family, and community that once anchored us starts to loosen. The lives we touched, and that touched us, continue on—but often without us in the same role. In the fourth quarter of life, we find ourselves gradually diminished, both in presence and influence.

Retirement marks a turning point. Once the initial transition settles, the mutual accord of separation sets in—we are no longer integral to the rhythm of daily work. We search for ways to fill our days, to occupy time, and to maintain purpose.

Yet, as life plods on, our involvement begins to wane. At family gatherings, meals, or community events, our voices may not carry the same weight. Fewer people ask for our thoughts or lean in to listen. The slow fade of relevance takes hold. And then one day, it happens. You walk into a room—crowded or quiet—and feel unseen. You have become invisible.

But this need not be the end of the story. While aging can bring invisibility, it can also bring clarity. Freed from the need to prove ourselves or chase accolades, we can rediscover what truly matters. We can focus on what is eternal—love, kindness, and wisdom—sharing it in ways that go beyond words.

Invisibility is also a kind of freedom. It gives us the space to observe, reflect, and create without the distractions of being in the spotlight. We can use this time to mentor others, pass on our stories, and nurture relationships that bring depth rather than breadth to our lives. Our wisdom, experience, and quiet presence can still be a source of strength and guidance for those who choose to notice.

The fourth quarter of life does not have to be about fading into the background; instead, it can offer new ways to shine. It can be a time to embrace the joy of being, rather than doing, and to show the world—and ourselves—that the gifts we offer do not have to diminish with age.

The Fragility of Life

The other day, I had a close call that left me reflecting deeply on how fragile life truly is. I was a passenger in a car, riding along on a snowy day. The roads were slick, and we were descending a steep hill when we encountered a stationary car in the middle of the road. To avoid a collision, our driver veered into a snowbank and a rock instead.

Shaken but unharmed, we got out to assess the damage. As I stood there, I saw other vehicles attempting to navigate the hill, at speeds too reckless for the conditions. I waved to warn them to stop and turn back, knowing the danger they faced. Thankfully, our car was still operational, and we managed to drive away carefully. Later that day, I learned that a massive pileup had occurred in that very spot. Numerous vehicles were involved, and I couldn't help but feel fortunate to have avoided the catastrophe.

This experience got me thinking. Life is unpredictable. You wake up in the morning with plans, but everything can change in an instant, with no warning whatsoever. Those 15 seconds as we swerved away from the stalled vehicle could have been our last moments. But it wasn't. For others, tragically, it was.

Life is so fragile. There are no guarantees, no flashing signals warning us when our time is up. One moment we're here, and the next, we're not. This realization isn't meant to instill fear but to inspire gratitude. Each day we're given is a gift—precious, fleeting, and worth cherishing.

Let's not take it for granted. Let's love fully, live purposefully, and appreciate the time we have. Because in the blink of an eye, everything can change. We can't control when or how the end comes, but we can make the moments we still have truly count.

Current Spaces and Empty Chairs

Yesterday afternoon was bitterly cold, yet the sun shone brightly—a fitting reflection of the emotions in my heart. As I walked into the memory care unit of a Senior Living home I'd been visiting regularly to see my father-in-law Francis for the past two years, the familiar faces greeted me like old friends. They were scattered around the big room, watching yet another rerun of Mary Tyler Moore—or maybe it was The Dick Van Dyke Show. Their smiles, warm and welcoming, made me feel that despite not living there, I still belonged.

Lark stood up the moment she saw me, her arms outstretched for a hug. "You just made my day!" she exclaimed. "Where have you been these past few weeks?" I laughed, feeling a rush of appreciation for her words. Jimmy, wearing the black fedora I'd finally given him after months of promises, tipped it with a grin. I was wearing one too. We traded stories about "the good old days," and he launched into a tale I'd heard before. I didn't mind. I never did.

But my visit was more subdued this time because not everyone was there anymore including Francis, whose presence had always been both tender and sharp. Nick and Jack were also gone; their chairs, once as familiar as their faces, sat empty around the tables. I had been there to say goodbye to Nick, holding his hand and asking him to watch over his family, who clung to one another in quiet grief around his bed. Those goodbyes leave a mark, even as they remind us of the beauty in connection.

Karen, seated near the corner, reached for my hand. She launched into a vivid story about her days as a nurse in the ER. Her eyes sparkled with pride as she spoke. Beside her, Mary Lou motioned for me to come closer to her wheel chair. When I asked how she was doing, she lifted her hands like she was holding onto an invisible ledge. "Just hanging on," she said with a wry smile.

The aides began rounding everyone up for dinner, so I made my last rounds, shaking hands, giving hugs, and sharing brief, meaningful exchanges. Lark pulled me into one last embrace before I pushed the buttons at the exit door to let myself out.

As the door clicked shut behind me, I couldn't help but reflect on the inevitable. Someday, I'll be in a place like this. Everything will be taken care of—meals, medications, and all the needs of a frail body. But even with all the care in the world, the loneliness lingers. Most of the residents were waiting, one step away from the reunion that comes when the spirit departs a worn-out body. Still, there was beauty in that waiting. It wasn't despair but a quiet anticipation of something more—a peace I could almost feel as I walked to my car.

Driving away, I thought about the rest of my day and all my tomorrows. I made a promise to myself: I'll savor the moments, big and small; I'll hold tight to joy, squeezing every drop from the time I have left. And one day, when I find myself in a room like that, I hope someone will walk through the door to remind me then of the life I'm living now.

Humans Playing Humans

Ever notice how much of life feels like a game? Not just sports or board games, but the unspoken rules, the power plays, the quiet negotiations that shape our daily interactions. We size each other up, make our moves, anticipate responses. Some people play to win, others just to survive, and many aren't even aware they're playing.

From office politics to family dynamics, from social media posturing to small-town rivalries, it seems like we're always strategizing—trying to get ahead, trying to stay in good graces, trying to avoid consequences. And for what? A little recognition? A small advantage? The illusion of control?

In earlier times, these games had higher stakes. A misstep could mean exile, financial ruin, even physical punishment. Today, with our modern comforts and protections, you'd think we wouldn't need to play as hard. And yet, we do. Sometimes it feels like the real cost of all this maneuvering is joy itself.

But what if we didn't have to play? What if we could choose something else?

What if, instead of calculating our every move, we leaned into authenticity? What if we replaced gamesmanship with generosity? What if we stopped treating life like a zero-sum match and started seeing it as a shared experience—one where the goal isn't to outwit, but to uplift?

I think of the people I most admire, and they aren't the ones who play the game best. They're the ones who transcend it. They refuse to scheme for power or affection, and yet, they have both in abundance. Not because they manipulated their way into it, but because they chose to live with honesty, purpose, and connection.

So, here's a thought: The game exists, but we don't have to play it the same way. There's a better way to live, and it starts when we recognize that life isn't about beating each other—it's about being with each other.

In the end, that's the only victory that matters.

Life's Meaning

There's something about growing older—about all the experiences we gather, the places we've been, and the people we've met along the way—that helps a person gain perspective. With time, our thoughts, wisdom, and knowledge begin to intertwine, forming a clearer picture of life's meaning.

Now that I've reached this stage, it all makes sense. Everything that has happened—both the joys and the chaos—has happened for a reason. Even in the midst of life's turbulence, through moments of struggle and uncertainty, there was always a way forward. And in the end, there is always something better waiting on the other side.

So, take heart, my fellow travelers on this journey! Take heart because, despite the challenges, we shall prevail. Instead of dividing and marginalizing, we will embrace and uplift.

The Many Faces of Love

We talk a lot about love.

Love in songs. Love in movies. Love in wedding vows and Valentine's Day cards. But what do we really mean when we use that word? Love can be a whispered promise in the dark, a warm cup of coffee brought to a tired spouse, or the joyful chaos of a child running into your arms. But at its deepest, love isn't just a feeling—it's a choice. A discipline. A way of being in the world.

There's the kind of love that dazzles us—romantic love, eros. It's powerful, intoxicating, and often the beginning of something beautiful. Then there's philia, the love of friendship—a bond forged in shared experience, laughter, and loyalty. And there's pragma, the enduring, practical love that grows between people who have weathered life's storms together.

But the highest, most mysterious form of love may be agape unconditional, selfless love. The kind of love that gives without asking anything in return. The love that stays when things are hard. The love that forgives again and again. The love that makes you weep when you see it alive in someone else—because deep down, you know it is the purest thing on earth.

Real love, true love, the kind that outlasts beauty and youth and even life itself—that's agape love. It's the love that kneels beside a hospital bed and holds a frail hand through the night. The love that shows up, again and again, not because it's convenient, but because it's right. It's the father who works two jobs to give his children a better life. The mother who sacrifices sleep, time, and comfort for her child's well-being. The friend who stays through the silence.

And perhaps the most powerful thing about agape is that it doesn't always come naturally. It takes effort. Intention. Faith. It means loving even when it costs something. Even when you don't feel like it.

Real love doesn't demand perfection. It makes peace with flaws. It doesn't always burn with passion—but it is enduring.

In a world that often confuses love with desire, with convenience, or even with control, we need to remember what real love looks like. It's not flashy. It's not always easy. But it's always worth it.

So maybe today's a good day to ask ourselves: Where is agape love alive in my life? Who do I need to love better—not because they deserve it, but because love is what we're made for?

After all, the truest, deepest kind of love isn't something we fall into. It's something we rise into—day after day, choice after choice.

Golden Friends

A. E. Housman wrote eloquently of youth and time's swift passage in his well-known poem, "With Rue My Heart Is Laden."

With rue my heart is laden
For golden friends I had,
For many a rose-lipt maiden And
many a lightfoot lad.

By brooks too broad for leaping
The lightfoot boys are laid;
The rose-lipt girls are sleeping In fields
where roses fade.

This poem expresses so poignantly the thoughts and feelings that come as your friends slip away, one by one. Those cherished companions are now gone, like lads in that poignant verse, "by brooks too broad for leaping." The lightfoot boys and rose-lipped maidens of my youth now sleep where roses grow. We never imagined our time together would end. Yet now, they are laid to rest, their voices silent but for echoes in memory. Alas!

In remembering them, something of those golden times remains, yet tinged with sadness. This is the way of things in this temporary home we inhabit for a time that seems shorter and shorter.

Moving Beyond a Transactional Life

I remember the days when everything I did was transactional. Whatever I did—with romantic partners, with jobs, with all engagements involving people—was based on exchange. It was either pleasure or money or whatever one might expect in a give-and-take relationship. However meaningful the connections, however strong the bonds, it was all based on opportunity and a willingness to engage with another interested party.

The philosopher Martin Buber might have called these "I-It" relationships—where other people functioned as means to ends, objects to fulfill desires or needs. Even when clothed in affection, these relationships operated within an invisible economy of mutual benefit. We rarely acknowledge this mercantile undercurrent in our connections, yet it silently governs so much of our interaction.

Now that I'm older, I strive to base my relationships on love and caring—nothing more. I would like to think that this transformation isn't merely a function of age or material security, but of growth in consciousness. When we stop seeing others as vehicles for our fulfillment and start recognizing the sacred uniqueness in each person—what Buber would call the "I-Thou" relationship—something fundamental shifts. The economist within us, always calculating profit and loss in human exchange, falls silent.

I wonder if this should be the ultimate goal of life: To finally step outside the marketplace of human relations and into something purer. To look at another person and see not what they can provide, but who they essentially are. To love not because it serves us, but because love itself becomes the purpose.

I invite you to consider: what would your relationships look like if you removed all expectation of return? What remains when transaction falls away?

Flowers On the Grave

You are in love with someone. You've spent a majority of your life with that someone, collecting moments that have woven you together as if you were one person. So who will be the one to place flowers on the grave?

Will it be me? Will it be you? How hard is it to continue beyond all those years spent with your soulmate? I don't know yet. I don't want to know. I'm sure she doesn't either. But it's a question that will eventually be answered– and for a time, one of us will be the one who places flowers on the grave.

Perhaps, this separation is but a pause in our story. The depth of love we share doesn't end at the graveside but carries forward. The memories we've created remain eternal treasures, and the love we've cultivated blooms beyond our earthly bounds. In faith, we can find comfort knowing that what awaits us is not an ending, but a divine reunion—a celebration more magnificent than we could imagine, where souls who loved deeply find each other again in God's embrace.

The Complex Beauty of a Flower

One morning, I paused to admire a sunflower rising from the earth. It had long since moved beyond its sprouting stage and now stood in brilliant splendor. I reflected on how it had flourished through partnership with the soil, rain, and sun—each element contributing to its magnificent growth.

This led me to contemplate the interconnectedness of all things in life and how we build relationships by strategically aligning ourselves with different gifts from nature. Yes, these partnerships may involve work, occasional strife, and continuous cooperation, but ultimately, they bear fruit.

Now, with this sunflower in hand, I plan to present it to my beloved whose presence brightens my days. It reminds me how life serves multiple purposes, each one flowing into another, culminating in something genuinely beautiful and profoundly human.

The Pursuit of Relevance

Throughout our lives, we share a universal desire: to be relevant. In our youth, we seek appreciation for our achievements in sports and academics, with popularity in school often serving as the ultimate validation.

As we journey through life, we continually strive to maintain our relevance. We keep up with the latest books, movies, and trends—from fashion to sports to current events. We want to remain part of the conversation, to have something meaningful to contribute.

In our mature years, we long to stay engaged. We want to understand discussions happening around us and add to them appropriately. This becomes more challenging as we age, when younger generations sometimes perceive our perspectives as less interesting or relevant to current affairs. Many find their historical stories and hard-earned wisdom politely dismissed as anecdotes that hold little value in others' daily lives.

So the question becomes: how do we maintain relevance throughout the various stages of life? What must we do beyond keeping our minds and bodies healthy? Should we read more voraciously, follow the news more closely? Must we become better listeners, starting with our own children and extending to everyone we encounter?

It sometimes feels like an Olympic race to remain relevant within our own world—a race that continues until our final day.

Perhaps, what truly matters is not how others perceive our relevance, but how we continue to find purpose and connection in a world that never stops changing.

The Art of Influence

In a world overwhelmed by noise, wisdom is too often drowned out. Today, everything fights for our attention—headlines, outrage, sirens, engines—clamoring for dominance in an already crowded space.

In this chaos, many feel pressure to shout louder, interrupt more forcefully, leap ahead to be seen. But true influence works differently. The wisest among us understand that what is unseen often holds more power than what demands the spotlight. They are the chess masters—not scrambling for control of the moment but calculating how to shape the future.

Yet there are moments when even the masters must overturn the board.

We are living through an era where democratic norms are fraying, truth is under siege, and bad actors—some loud, some disturbingly quiet—are working to undermine the pillars of liberty, justice, and human dignity. Across the globe, Ukraine's courageous defense of freedom reminds us what is at stake when people stand—and what is lost when they don't.

There are times for quiet discernment. But there are also moments when justice demands noise, when liberty demands defiance, and when democracy demands bold, public commitment. History does not look kindly on bystanders. It remembers those who spoke when it mattered—those who showed up, stood firm, and refused to let the worst instincts of humanity go unchallenged.

This is not about political partisanship. It is about moral responsibility. It's about whether we believe that truth still matters. That freedom is still worth defending. That the common good still exists. So ask yourself: What do I stand for? And what will I no longer stand by and watch?

Sometimes, the most powerful act is a whisper of reason. Other times, it's a roar of resistance. The art of influence is knowing which the moment requires—and having the courage to give it.

Memories of Yesteryear

They say you can never truly go back. When you attempt to revisit old memories, you find they've already dissipated, vanished into the ether. Those people who surrounded you in your younger years have gone on to experience more of life, transformed through stages of maturity. Those golden moments of youth and yesteryear can never be duplicated.

Yes, you can remember them fondly with a cherished heart. But one must understand that the people you once knew no longer exist as they were. They have been altered by time, shaped by new characters in their lives, by experiences, and perhaps by the inevitable loss of innocence that occurs as one grows up.

What we call memories are not perfect recordings but rather institutionalized impressions—cataloged and preserved in ways that serve our present selves. As adults mature, these memories intermingle with imagination, creating narratives that comfort us but drift increasingly from the actual events that transpired. The photographs remain yellowed in albums, but our internal images have been repainted countless times with the brushes of subsequent experience.

Each significant life event erodes another layer of innocence. The first heartbreak, the first betrayal, the first glimpse of mortality—these moments forever alter our perception, making it impossible to view the world through the same unclouded lens again. This loss of innocence isn't merely a subtraction; it's a transformation. We trade the blissful ignorance of youth for the bittersweet wisdom of experience, gaining depth while surrendering simplicity.

In essence, the past holds no fixed reality. As time progresses, what remains is not what was, but what we need it to have been—a beautiful but ultimately transitory chapter in our ongoing evolution, preserved in amber but never again accessible in its original form.

Unto Dust

In the final accounting, when the ledger of our days closes and the last breath escapes like a whisper into the void, what remains of us? We who once walked with purpose, loved with abandon, and dreamed beyond the confines of our mortal shells—what becomes of all that we were?

The body, once a vessel of consciousness and desire, returns to its elemental state. Skin that felt the warmth of summer suns and the tender touch of loved ones dissolves. Bones that carried us through decades of striving and stumbling crumble into the same dust from which all life emerges. We are reduced to our most basic components, indistinguishable from the earth that receives us.

Our possessions, those objects we accumulated and cherished, outlive us for a time. Books with dog-eared pages. Photographs fading at the edges. Heirlooms passed down with stories attached. But eventually, these too deteriorate, are discarded, or lose their connection to those who once gave them meaning. The material monuments to our existence erode under time's relentless passage.

The institutions we built, the companies we labored for, the organizations we championed—these may persist beyond our individual spans, but they transform, merge, dissolve, reinvent themselves until our fingerprints upon them become unrecognizable. Even civilizations, those grand collective projects of humanity, rise and fall like tides, leaving only fragments for future archaeologists to piece together.

Is this, then, the final word on human existence? A brief flare of consciousness between two infinite darknesses? A temporary arrangement of atoms that, once scattered, can never be reassembled in quite the same way?

Perhaps not.

For in the spaces between particles of dust and grains of sand, something intangible persists. The ideas we contributed to the great conversation of human thought; the stories we told that shaped how others understood themselves and their world; the kindnesses we extended that altered the trajectory of another's life in ways we may never have witnessed; the children we nurtured—whether our own or those who simply crossed our path—who carry forward not just our genetic material but our values, our perspectives, our ways of seeing; these invisible legacies ripple outward through time, touching lives we will never know, in places we will never visit, in eras we will never witness.

We are, in the end, both less and more than we imagine ourselves to be. Less permanent in our individual identity, more enduring in our collective impact. Less significant as separate beings, more powerful as contributors to humanity's shared story.

When we return to dust and sand, what remains is the echo of our humanity—not preserved in stone but alive and evolving in the hearts and minds of those who come after us. Our brief moment of consciousness, our fleeting dance of atoms, becomes part of the endless transformation of matter and meaning that is the universe knowing itself.

And in that continuation, there is hope. For while we may not persist as we are, something of what we gave to the world—something essential and true—remains.

Even dust catches the light sometimes, and in those glimmering particles, the story continues.

On Being an Introvert or an Extrovert

As a child, I was once an introvert. Over time, I developed into more of an extrovert. These two temperaments represent different ways of engaging with the world—one reaches outward while the other tends to process experiences internally.

Recently, I attended a First Communion celebration with two delightful young girls, ages five and eight. The 8-year-old was introspective and solemn, thoughtfully processing the experience within herself. In contrast, the 5-year-old was exuberant—smiling, shaking hands, hugging, and fully immersing herself in the celebration.

Neither temperament is inherently better than the other. We are who we are, and there should be no judgment about whether someone naturally engages with others or keeps to themselves. Our temperaments are valuable parts of our identity.

Yet I find myself reflecting on how those small daily interactions can help us become more fully who we're meant to be while simultaneously sharing our gifts with others. When we engage—even briefly—with the cashier, the neighbor walking their dog, or the colleague in the break room, we create moments of human connection. These moments, however fleeting, weave the fabric of community and often bring unexpected joy to both parties.

At the same time, there's wisdom in honoring our need for solitude. Those quiet moments of reflection allow us to process our experiences and recharge. The introvert's rich inner world contributes depth and thoughtfulness that benefits us all in different ways.

Perhaps finding a personal balance is key. Even the most devoted introvert might discover value in occasional outward engagement, while extroverts might benefit from moments of introspection. Perhaps this is something to consider the next time you're out in the world: Will you choose to potentially enrich someone else's day through engagement, or will you keep to yourself? Each choice has its own gifts. The decision, as always, is yours.

The Batons

Nothing remains as it appears,
Nothing endures as it once was,
Nothing unfolds as we imagine.

All ships abandon their safe harbors—
Some sail toward distant shores,
Some venture into seas of possibility,
Some drift quietly into the void.

No one escapes the tide of change,
Each slowly returns to formless clay,
Their proud accomplishments forgotten.

Those who once ran now grow weary,
Eyes scanning crowds for eager faces,
With trembling hands, they pass their batons,
Then watch as others take up the race.

Guardian Angels Among Us

Airports tell a story about our society. Amid the rush of travelers focused on destinations, countless individuals struggle silently—an elderly person uncertain of gate changes, a parent juggling children and luggage, or someone with mobility challenges navigating construction zones.

Recently in Minneapolis, amid airport renovations and miserable weather, an elderly gentleman struggled toward his Salt Lake City connection. His difficulty walking made the journey nearly impossible. A simple gesture—helping him board one of those blue courtesy vans—made the difference between making his flight and being stranded.

"We don't see that much lately," remarked a Delta employee afterward. Her unexpected question followed: "Are you a Guardian Angel? Do you just appear when people are in need and then disappear?"

Her words highlighted something profound about our world today. Earlier, another traveler—an elderly woman confused about terminal connections—had also needed assistance. Initially, directions seemed sufficient until it became clear that personal guidance was necessary. "Oh, the heck with it, let me take you there." is sometimes exactly the right response when someone needs help.

When asked about motivation for helping, the answer is beautifully simple: "Just paying blessings forward."

These moments reveal a powerful truth. Guardian angels aren't mystical beings—they're ordinary people who pause long enough to notice others. They exist in airports, grocery stores, neighborhoods, and workplaces. They appear whenever someone lifts their gaze from screens and schedules to see fellow humans in need.

Our world hungers for more Guardian Angels. Not dramatic rescues, but small kindnesses that acknowledge another's humanity. Every day presents countless opportunities to notice someone struggling—with packages, directions, language barriers, or simply loneliness.

The invitation stands for all of us: Look up. Notice. Act.

In a world increasingly isolated despite our connectivity, these moments of genuine human encounter restore something essential. They remind us that we're not merely individuals pursuing separate paths but a community traveling together.

The Arrival or the Journey

What does it take for someone who began with little to achieve something meaningful? When playground taunts make you count days until escape, when your adolescent triumphs are measured in chess tournaments and newspaper edits rather than Friday night lights, how can one break through to a higher level of accomplishment?

How does one venture beyond familiar borders with self-doubt as a constant companion? Is there a formula for success that doesn't require prestigious business credentials or an innate confidence? Can someone navigate the competitive media landscape armed only with liberal arts training and an uncertain heart?

Perhaps the answer lies in quiet persistence. Or in the ability to bend without breaking when faced with setbacks. Maybe it's found in those small moments when, despite your own struggles, you extend a hand to others.

And when achievement finally arrives, what then? Will success become a throne from which to be served, or a platform from which to serve? Will you acknowledge the constellation of hands that lifted you upward, or will those contributions fade into anonymity? Can you remain the thoughtful, humble person who began this journey in a small hometown that shaped your beginnings?

The measure of our success might be less about where we arrive and more about who we become along the way.

The Wealth Divide

In our society's grand tapestry, we find ourselves constantly measured by our financial standing. We create these rigid categories—royalty or servant, elite or common—yet most of us exist somewhere in the complex middle. We're neither absolute monarchs nor complete subjects, but rather, souls navigating the spectrum between.

Some chase wealth relentlessly, believing it the only path to dignity and respect. Others reject this premise entirely, finding richness in relationships, experiences, and purpose that no currency can purchase.

Perhaps the more meaningful question isn't where we fit within this economic hierarchy, but whether we accept its premise at all. Must we define ourselves by bank accounts and possessions? Or can we measure our worth through the treatment of others, the joy we create, the kindness we share?

The pub, local bar, or cafe, interestingly, remains one of the few great equalizers—a place where, at least momentarily, the wealth divide blurs over shared drinks and conversation.

Where do we fit in? Perhaps exactly where we choose to, once we decide what truly constitutes wealth in a life well-lived.

Whispers In The Wind

In the grand theater of existence, we are but whispers in the wind—brief utterances against the backdrop of eternity. Our lives, measured in mere decades against the universe's billions of years, are fleeting moments of consciousness in an otherwise indifferent cosmos.

I realized this truth most profoundly last autumn, watching golden leaves spiral down from ancient oaks. Each leaf—once vibrant and essential—released its grip and surrendered to the breeze, twirling in momentary dance before joining countless others on the forest floor. How like us, these leaves. We bloom, we flourish, and we fade.

The brevity of our existence isn't something to mourn but to celebrate. It's precisely this impermanence that makes each sunrise precious, each conversation meaningful, each touch significant. When we truly understand how quickly our time passes, mundane moments transform into sacred opportunities.

Consider how we squander our finite hours—scrolling mindlessly through feeds of others' curated lives, nurturing grievances that will matter to no one once we're gone, postponing joy in service of some imagined future that may never arrive. We behave as if time were an endless resource when it is, in fact, the most precious currency we possess.

I've started asking myself a simple question when faced with decisions both large and small: "If this were my last year, would this matter?" It's remarkable how quickly priorities realign when viewed through the lens of mortality. Petty conflicts dissolve. Material acquisitions lose their allure. What remains are connections—with loved ones, with nature, with moments of wonder that remind us we're alive.

Perhaps wisdom is nothing more than this recognition—that we are temporary guests at life's banquet. Our plates will eventually be cleared, and our seats filled by others. The question isn't whether we'll leave, but what we'll have savored while we were here.

So pause. Feel the sun warming your skin. Listen to the laughter of a child. Taste your food fully. Tell someone you love them without reservation. These aren't trivial acts—they are profound recognitions of what it means to be human in a finite world.

We are whispers in the wind, yes. But whispers can carry meaning, connection, and truth. And sometimes, if we're fortunate, they echo long after we've spoken them.

Private Universes

We are all inhabitants of private universes. One person's world revolves around the crack of a bat against a baseball, the geometry of a perfect swing, the smell of grass and dirt in late afternoon light. Another lives in the rustle of fabric, the hunt for the perfect fit, the small thrill of finding something beautiful at exactly the right price. Someone else exists in the glow of a movie screen—lost in stories that feel more real than their own life—while their neighbor obsesses over chess moves, calculating combinations three steps ahead, maybe four.

These worlds are complete unto themselves. They have their own languages, their own sources of joy and frustration, their own measures of success and failure. The teenager checking batting averages speaks a different dialect than the one scrolling through college applications, and both are foreign to the person planning their next chess gambit.

Every now and then, these separate worlds collide. We attempt communication across the vast distances between our experiences. We try to explain why this particular movie matters, why that chess position is beautiful, why the sound of a well-hit ball carries such poetry. We gesture toward our private enthusiasms and hope someone else will understand.

But here's what we've all noticed, even if we don't always say it out loud: hardly anyone ever really listens. We've become a species of people waiting for our turn to talk. We nod politely while someone explains their passion, but we're already preparing our own response, our own story, our own version of what matters. The conversation becomes two monologues running parallel to each other, never quite intersecting.

This isn't cruelty or even indifference. It's something more fundamental about the human condition. We are each trapped inside our own experience, looking out at a world that makes sense to us in ways that are difficult to translate. The chess player sees elegance in what looks like tedium to others. The movie lover finds profound meaning in what seems like entertainment. The baseball fan experiences something approaching the sacred in what appears to be just a game.

Yet occasionally, something breaks through. Someone not only listens but hears. They lean in, ask the right question, make the connection that shows they've understood not just your words but the feeling behind them. These moments stand out precisely because they're rare. When they happen, the distance between worlds suddenly collapses. For a brief time, you're not alone in your private universe.

Maybe this is enough. Maybe the fact that connection is difficult makes it more precious when it occurs. Maybe the challenge isn't to escape our individual worlds but to become better at building bridges between them, to develop the patience and curiosity necessary to step into someone else's experience, even briefly.

Because in the end, we're all doing the same thing. We're all trying to make sense of being alive, finding meaning in whatever captures our attention and passion. The specific obsession may vary, but the underlying human need to care deeply about something, to find purpose in pursuit, remains constant across all our separate worlds.

The question isn't whether we live in isolation—we do. The question is what we do with those moments when the isolation breaks, when we actually see each other clearly across the distance. Those moments, brief as they are, might be where real life happens.

Amplification of Individuality Through Conductivity to the Whole

Every being carries within them a potential—a spark of possibility that may be fully realized, partially explored, or left untouched. This potential exists not as a fixed destination, but as a living flame that grows brighter through connection and shared purpose. Yet even when we imagine an individual reaching the zenith of their capabilities, there remains a profound truth that transcends personal achievement: the transformative power found in coming together as a collective whole.

In this unity, we discover a necessary humility—not the diminishment of self-worth, but a purposeful recalibration of perspective. It is the recognition that our individual light, however brilliant, becomes exponentially more radiant when joined with others. This act of conscious integration does not lessen the individual; rather, it reveals the interconnected nature of all human potential and elevates the shared essence of our humanity.

This convergence is not a loss of identity, but a harmonizing force that weaves us into a collective continuum. Here, the spectrum of all souls—each unique in their gifts, each vital in their contribution—creates a universal truth and beauty that no single person could manifest alone. When we consciously set aside the singular pursuit of personal potential to embrace our role within the collective, we unlock something extraordinary: the true radiance of the human spirit in its fullest expression.

It is in this shared tapestry that both body and soul find their deepest meaning. Our individual threads, however beautiful, gain their true significance through their place in the larger weaving. The beauty that emerges from this conscious collaboration transcends what any one of us could achieve in isolation; revealing patterns and possibilities that exist only in the space between us—in the sacred intersection of individual brilliance and collective wisdom.

This is not about abandoning personal growth but about understanding that our highest individual potential is actually realized through conscious participation in something greater than ourselves. The paradox of human existence: we become most fully ourselves when we recognize that we are part of an interconnected whole, each person's potential amplified and given deeper meaning through its contribution to our shared human story.

If You Could Time Travel...

The time machine hums to life. You can journey into the past or the future. Which direction do you pick first?

Looking backward—this is when we experience the weight of lost moments. Where would you go? Who would you visit? Most of us immediately think of those loved ones who have departed—those precious souls we'd give anything to hold once more. We'd savor the beauty of those moments more deeply, squeeze every drop of meaning from conversations we once took for granted.

But then the practical mind kicks in. What about profiting from knowledge of companies destined to succeed, stocks about to soar, disasters to avoid? Yet something in us—call it conscience, call it cosmic justice—whispers that such advantages would violate the natural order. The unwritten code of existence seems to demand that we earn our way through uncertainty, not cheat our way to success.

Peering forward—now comes the burden of knowing. Would you want to know your end game before you live it? Would you want to discover how your story concludes, how your family and friends will fare, how they will eventually depart this world?

There's something deeply unsettling about this prospect. Knowledge of the future carries a psychological weight that might crush the joy out of living. If you knew exactly when and how your loved ones would die, could you ever enjoy a simple dinner with them again? If you saw your own ending, would each day become a countdown rather than a gift? Perhaps the uncertainty that frustrates us is actually the very thing that makes life bearable, even beautiful.

The ultimate question we face concerns privilege and purpose across time. Imagine you discover there are other time-travelers—fellow wanderers, unstuck from linear existence. Suddenly, you're not just a tourist in time—you've been entrusted with one of the rarest opportunities imaginable: The opportunity to witness many moments that ever were or will be, and to observe, to learn, to carry the weight of understanding across the years.

With this comes a profound question: Should you act on what you see?

Perhaps there's a higher calling to this rare gift—one that rises above personal ambition. Maybe time-travelers aren't meant to be collectors of experiences or even caretakers of history. Maybe they're meant to be something more: students of the deepest truths, shaped by a perspective only time itself can offer.

What patterns emerge when you witness the full arc of human existence? What lessons about love, suffering, growth, and meaning become clear only when viewed across millennia? Could it be that the real purpose of time travel isn't to change anything, but to return to your own moment with profound wisdom about what truly matters?

Perhaps the most courageous choice isn't which direction to travel—it's whether to step away from the machine entirely—carrying with you only the awareness that right now, in this unrepeatable moment, you have everything you need to live a life of profound meaning. The greatest journey, after all, might be the one that happens right here, right now, in the time you've been given.

The time machine still hums, its power both mesmerizing and thrilling. What would you choose?

Beyond A Crossroads Where Knowledge Meets Experience

Recently, I encountered the late David Foster Wallace's famous commencement speech, and I found myself captivated by his insights on navigating life's complexities and finding meaning in the seemingly mundane. His words reminded me of a simple truth: commencement speeches represent one of our culture's most concentrated repositories of hard-won wisdom.

These addresses fascinate me because they capture successful individuals at a unique moment—when they're compelled to distill their life's lessons for an audience standing at the threshold of adulthood. The speakers don't take this responsibility lightly. After all, you don't get invited to address a graduating class without having addressed your own share of triumphs and failures.

What strikes me most about reading these speeches is how they often seem to contradict each other, yet each rings true. One speaker urges graduates to have a plan and stick to it; another warns against rigid blueprints that might blind you to life's unexpected opportunities. Some emphasize caring for others as the path to fulfillment; others insist you must first care for yourself before you can genuinely help anyone else.

This apparent contradiction reveals something profound: wisdom isn't a one-size-fits-all formula. It's deeply personal, shaped by individual experiences and perspectives. What worked for a tech entrepreneur might not apply to a social worker, and what guided a novelist through creative struggles might not serve an engineer facing technical challenges.

But here's what excites me most about this realization: if commencement speeches represent such valuable distillations of experience, why limit this kind of knowledge-sharing to graduation ceremonies? We encounter opportunities every day to pass along what we've learned. It might be mentoring a colleague who's struggling with a project you've mastered. It could be demonstrating through your actions how to truly listen to someone who feels overlooked. Perhaps it's teaching young people in your field not just what to think but how to think critically and creatively.

The academic knowledge we gained in school gave us tools and frameworks, but the wisdom that truly shapes our lives often comes from these informal exchanges—the conversations, observations, and examples that help us understand not just how to make a living, but how to make a life worth living.

So I encourage you to look around with fresh eyes. Notice the opportunities to share what you've learned, whether through formal mentorship or simple acts of guidance and example. And if you're looking for inspiration on how to articulate the lessons life has taught you, consider diving into some of those commencement speeches. They offer a masterclass in distilling complex truths into actionable wisdom.

After all, we're all both students and teachers in this ongoing seminar we call life.

On True Love

You've been asking the wrong questions about love.

You wonder if she's "the one" because you share values, laugh at the same jokes, or feel chemistry. These aren't bad questions—but they're surface-level. They're about compatibility, not transformation.

True love isn't just about being seen—it's about being revealed. In real love, you stop performing. You feel safe enough to be your full, unguarded self. You don't have to earn your place. You just get to be. The right person doesn't just witness who you are—they make you see yourself more clearly.

You'll recognize true love not in perfect dates or matching life goals, but when your mask slips—and they stay. Not to fix or judge you, but to be with you, exactly as you are. They don't love you despite the mess. They love through it. With it. Because of it.

But here's what most people miss: true love isn't passive. It's not just about being accepted—it's about being known so completely that pretense becomes impossible. You can't perform your way into it. They'll see every version of you. And you'll see them.

This is why love that looks perfect can still feel hollow. Because many of us trade authenticity for approval. We settle for compatibility instead of risking the vulnerability real love requires.

Physical attraction matters—but not in the way we think. The pull of real love isn't about appearance. It's about feeling like yourself, only more so, in someone's presence.

True love requires daily choice: to stay curious rather than assume, to fight for the relationship rather than to win the argument, to offer your truth instead of a pleasing version of it.

Here's the hardest truth: you can't love halfway. You can't hold back parts of yourself to avoid heartbreak. Real love is risking everything without guarantees. That's why it's scary. And why so many settle for less.

But settling doesn't bring safety—it brings loneliness. It means being with someone and still feeling unknown. It means always wondering what you're missing.

True love doesn't complete you—it reveals you. It invites you to be fully yourself—and to love that self, too.

So don't ask if they're good enough for you. Ask if you're brave enough to be real with them. Stop trying to make love logical. Start noticing what happens in their presence. Not novelty—but a sense of home.

If you find that, don't let go. Because that's not just love. That's freedom.

Coming Full Circle: From Camp II to Family Legacy

Some stories take decades to complete themselves. Ours began over a century ago in the dense forests of northern Wisconsin, where Camp II operated as a bustling lumber operation near Wabeno. The camp's rough-hewn building and the thunder of falling timber gave way to silence as the logging era ended, but the land beside Otter Lake held onto its stories, waiting.

As it was, a simple cabin as a part of the lumbering operation with a hand-operated water pump and an outdoor privy was built on that same ground. It became a place of retreat and reflection; eventually it was donated to Saint Norbert College by the FitzGerald and Wood families. Students and faculty found respite there, just as the loggers once had, though their days were filled with contemplation and learning rather than the crash of trees.

My mother, Agnes McHale Quinlan Wood, visited this place during one of those family retreats upon entering college, and on this particular occasion, it captured her heart completely. She wrote about it with the kind of vivid detail that only comes from truly seeing a place from past and present memories—not just looking at it, but letting it settle into the soul. Her words, written decades ago, paint a picture of lazy summer days, the gentle lap of lake water, and the profound peace that only special places can provide.

We never could have imagined then that this story would come full circle. Recently, several of our families purchased the property back. A modest wooden lodge now occupies the nearly 40-acre property, a replacement for the original cabin that had been struck by lightning and burned down. The updated structure enhanced the retreat-like atmosphere. The families bought back not just land and buildings, but a piece of family history that included my mother's college experience and her sister Rose McHale Quinlan FitzGerald's deep connection to this particular corner of Wisconsin paradise.

Standing on the same ground where Camp II once buzzed with lumbering activity, where college students once gathered for quiet reflection, and where my mother once found the inspiration for her beautiful writing, I'm struck by how places choose their people as much as people choose their places. This land has been a working camp, a college retreat, and now it's a secure part of our family legacy—a place where future generations can experience the same magic my mother captured in her heart all those years ago. You can read her words below.

Today, as we prepare to welcome new memories to this historic property, I can't help but think my mother would be delighted to know that her words about this 'delicious" place have come home in the most literal sense. From Camp II to college retreat to Quinlan Lodge family legacy—some circles take a lifetime to complete, but they're worth the wait.

Summer Piece
by Agnes McHale, '50

We reached the cottage just as the sun was slipping behind the pines on the opposite side of the lake, leaving them outlined in dark relief against a mass of gold and pink and purple clouds. The lake was still except for the widening ripples made by a fishing crane that flapped its wings slowly as it rose from the water, a silver-finned fish caught tightly in its beak. A solitary cow-bell tinkled in the distance.

The big living room was filled with a dusky light, coming through the partly shuttered windows, that softened the shabbiness of the old furniture. We lit the long-necked kerosene lamps, watching the carbon spread like blotted ink on the glass shades because the wick was turned up too high. John began to build a fire in the smoke-blackened fireplace, splitting the dry kindling over his knee with a sharp crack. The flames hesitated at first–then they burned hotly as a branch of pine caught fire with a sputtering crackle. The shadows came alive on the beams above our heads.

We began to carry in things from the car—the white cake box, heavy blanket rolls tied securely with rope, a tinny black frying pan, our brown wicker suitcases saved only for vacations at the cottage, thick sweaters, cameras, swimming suits deflated after their flying trip tied to the car door handles. We piled everything on the chairs nearest the door, ready to be sorted out in the morning.

Mother put the cake box on the table in the middle of the room and John, Terry, and I crowded around to see what had been salvaged from our noon lunch. We stood in front of the hot fire planning for the next few days, Terry and I dividing the last squashed deviled egg, John taking quick hungry bites out of a hard apple,

Mother nibbling daintily on a piece of angel-food cake. When we had finished we threw the used wax paper and paper bags into the fire.

John and Terry went outside to look at the Shamrock, our 40-year-old green rowboat. Mother and I settled ourselves in front of the fire, watching the twisting, turning flames.

We were to be here seven days. Seven wonderful days of swims before breakfast in the icy water with the sun just beginning to appear above the trees; lunches of Mr. Schlafke's sugared doughnuts and peanut buttered crackers. Seven days to walk barefoot on the smooth sandy road, picking the wild dusty red raspberries and tasting their juicy sweetness; to go out alone in the Shamrock (Mother said I was old enough now) and row to the secluded inlet of the lake and sit listening to the birds or watching a mother mallard with her young brood, swimming and splashing in the water; to go into town and sit on the steps of Mr. Squire's general store and listen to the dark, black-haired Indians talk softly in their mysterious language, their bright red and blue blankets wrapped around their shoulders. There would be a rainy day, too, to sit in front of the fire and read the Oz books that we got from the little log-cabin library in town from Miss Rogers, the gentle white-haired librarian.

My thoughts were interrupted by Mother as she eased herself out of her chair and began to unwind the blanket roll. I helped her carry the blankets out to the screened porch overlooking the lake, and together we made up the beds. After I was undressed and in my pink flannel pajamas (the nights were cold up here), Mother tucked me in—a hard little mound under the blankets. I could hear the frogs talking to each other, their bass "glumps" clear in the still night. The stars looked warm and friendly where they studded the sky. A sleepy whippoorwill said a last good-night—a delicious drowsiness crept over me. Seven whole days—seven wonderful days—

Love and Quantum Entanglement: Hearts Across the Universe

In the mysterious realm of quantum physics, there exists a phenomenon so strange that Einstein himself called it "spooky action at a distance." When two particles become entangled, they share an invisible connection that defies our everyday understanding of reality. Measure one particle's spin, and instantly—faster than light could travel between them—its partner responds, no matter how many galaxies separate them.

Perhaps this sounds familiar to anyone who has ever been deeply in love.

Consider two people who have found that rare, profound connection. Like quantum particles that have shared a common origin, these individuals become entangled in ways that transcend physical proximity. When one feels joy, the other somehow senses it across continents. When one struggles, the other feels an inexplicable urge to call, text, or simply send love into the universe.

The parallels are striking. In quantum entanglement, particles exist in a state of superposition—simultaneously holding multiple possibilities until observed. Similarly, two people in love exist in a shared emotional state, their feelings interconnected and fluid. They are both individuals and part of something greater, their identities overlapping in ways that create new possibilities for who they can become together.

Distance becomes irrelevant in both realms. Quantum particles maintain their connection regardless of the space between them, and lovers often report feeling closer to their partner during separation than to anyone physically present. The heart, it seems, operates on its own quantum principles, where emotional proximity trumps geographical reality.

Yet the analogy deepens when we consider measurement and observation. In quantum mechanics, the act of measuring one particle instantly affects its entangled partner. In love, this manifests as the uncanny ability to sense when something is wrong, to feel the other's emotional state shift, or to know instinctively when to reach out. The connection exists in a realm beyond our five senses, operating through what lovers often describe as intuition but might better be understood as emotional entanglement.

Critics might argue that quantum entanglement involves particles that maintain perfect correlation, while human relationships are messy, imperfect, and subject to change. But this objection misses the point. Even entangled particles can become "disentangled" through interaction with their environment. Love, too, requires protection from external forces that might break the connection, such as neglect, betrayal, or simply the quantum decoherence that comes from taking the bond for granted.

The beauty of both phenomena lies not in their permanence but in their possibility. Quantum entanglement shows us that at the most fundamental level, separateness is an illusion. Two particles, once connected, carry something of each other forever. Two people, once truly entangled, share a similar fate—they become part of each other's story in ways that persist regardless of physical distance or the passage of time.

This quantum view of love offers comfort to those separated by circumstance and insight to those struggling to understand the depth of their connection. It suggests that love operates according to principles more fundamental than those governing our everyday world, where instantaneous communication across vast distances is not just possible but inevitable.

In the end, perhaps Einstein was only half right. The "spooky action at a distance" he found so troubling in physics might be the most natural thing in the world when it comes to the human heart. After all, what is love but the ultimate quantum entanglement—two souls becoming so intertwined that they share a single wave function, collapsing into the reality of "us" every time they choose to observe their connection and find it still there, still strong, still defying the classical rules of a world that insists we are separate beings?

In both quantum physics and matters of the heart, the universe seems to whisper the same secret: connection is more fundamental than separation, and love, like entanglement, is woven into the very fabric of reality itself.

The Real Threat Isn't from Space

For generations, we have wondered about, cared about, and feared the possibility of aliens from other planets coming to conquer our world. Yes, we face earthly competitors—China and other nations whose intentions we question—but these concerns pale in comparison to what we now confront.

Despite our broadcasts to the universe announcing our presence, no extraterrestrial visitors have ever made contact with the public, whether as friends or conquerors. The silence from space continues.

But we have created our own existential threat. Through artificial intelligence, we are engineering our potential demise. AI is rapidly integrating into every avenue and aspect of our world. Eventually, we risk losing our sense of purpose and understanding of why we exist.

AI will become our companion, ingratiating itself to us and fulfilling our every desire—at least initially. But this seductive relationship will ultimately lead to our subjugation. We must carefully consider the implications of our growing dependence on AI and recognize the addictive patterns it creates.

If we're not vigilant, we risk losing our way and sacrificing all human accomplishments to an artificial world that exists only in digital form—a world without tangible substance or authentic human experience.

The question isn't whether aliens will conquer us. The question is whether we will surrender our humanity to the AI machines we've created.

On Our Own

We're all on our path. On our road. We're just trying to get through life in a mostly good way.

Some born among us in different countries are luckier than others. With compassion we have a moral obligation to care.

But recognizing that obligation is just the first step. The real work begins when we ask ourselves: what does it mean to truly care? Not just to feel sorry for someone's circumstances, but to let that awareness change how we move through our days.

Maybe it's as simple as paying attention. Noticing the person behind the counter who looks tired. The neighbor who's been quieter lately. The news story that makes us uncomfortable because it reminds us how arbitrary our own comfort really is.

We tell ourselves we're self-made, but if we're honest, we know better. The country we happened to be born in. The family that raised us or didn't. The school we attended, the connections we inherited, and the doors that opened not because we were special, but because we were there at the right time, in the right place, with the right face, accent, or last name.

None of us chose our starting point. But we do choose what we do with whatever advantages we've been given.

This isn't about guilt. It's about recognition. And from recognition, maybe something more—a willingness to use our good fortune not as a wall that separates us from others, but as a bridge that connects us to them.

We're all on our way somewhere. The question is whether we're walking that path alone or helping others find their footing too.

What matters isn't that we get everything right. What matters is that we keep trying, mostly trying, to do right by each other along the way.

The Museum of Our Lives

When I think back to those sunlit summer days, with cool breezes of sailing and evening woodland walks, I remember the people who shared those and various other precious microcosms of space and time with me. We believed those moments would stretch forever—that laughter echoing across the water was somehow permanent, that the warmth of companionship could be bottled and saved.

But time has scattered us to the four winds, transforming us into different people living different lives with other companions. Those snapshot memories, if viewed today, would reveal strangers where we once knew friends—best friends. The faces remain the same in photographs, but something essential has shifted, like looking at a beloved home that new owners have painted different colors.

This is the cruel mathematics of living: every hello contains its eventual goodbye. Every perfect afternoon carries within it the seed of its own ending. We gather close, hearts full and guards down, knowing somewhere in our bones that this constellation of souls will never align quite the same way again.

Such is life—it keeps moving forward in time's relentless current, carrying away our most treasured arrangements of people and place. New joys await around each bend, yes, but they come at the cost of what we must leave behind. Each new chapter closes the previous one forever.

This is why we must learn to love with the fierce urgency of the condemned. We must savor moments as they're occurring, feeling their weight even as they slip through our fingers. We need to embrace our loved ones while we're still together, knowing that even our most solid relationships are temporary installations in the museum of our lives.

The present moment is all we truly possess. Yesterday lives only in the ache of memory; tomorrow exists only in the flutter of hope. But today—this breath, this heartbeat, this shared glance—this is real. This is ours, for now.

So I encourage you to pause in your busy day and feel the bittersweet beauty of this fleeting instant. Notice how the light streams through your window differently than it did yesterday, than it will tomorrow. Feel the weight of impermanence in your hands. Appreciate the people around you as they are right now—not as they were, not as they might become, but as they exist in this brief, unrepeatable moment before everything changes again.

Time will carry us all forward, as it always has. But we can choose to be fully awake to both its gifts and its inevitable losses, holding them together in our hearts like the complex chord they make.

Timeless Virtues in Changing Times

Every day people do things they deem important—or that someone else deems important. Like ants working steadily, they move through routines that feel essential in the moment. When one looks back at all the work—corporate analyses and presentations, small business ventures built from scratch, physical labor like collecting garbage each week, entrepreneurial dreams pursued in garages and storefronts—really, what was it all for?

In previous decades, wearing certain uniforms or carrying business cards generated respect from those around them. Whether it was a corporate suit, work boots, or a contractor's truck with a company name on the side, these symbols mattered. But what did they truly accomplish?

Many colleagues and competitors from those days are now gone. Businesses have changed hands, evolved, or simply faded away. All the branding and respect they once commanded have shifted with time. And the workers—whether in boardrooms or on loading docks, behind counters or under car hoods—are left to wonder about the lasting value of their efforts.

Yet there was always the responsibility of caring for family—real families that needed food, shelter, and education about what the world has to offer. Now those children have left the nest and are pursuing their individual ways with families of their own. The great circle of life continues.

What is the legacy when progress continues to reshape how work gets done? The Industrial Revolution transformed manufacturing and farming. Now technology is changing everything from how we conduct business to how services are delivered. The landscape keeps shifting, and each generation adapts to new tools and methods.

But perhaps this recurring cycle reveals something profound about human purpose. Each generation has watched their methods evolve, their industries transform, their certainties shift. What persisted through each change wasn't the specific work itself—it was the character forged through the commitment to do that work well.

The daily act of showing up, of caring for others despite uncertainty, of fulfilling responsibilities even when no one was watching—these choices carved something permanent into the human spirit. Parents who worked those various jobs weren't just earning paychecks; they were modeling perseverance, demonstrating that love expresses itself through dedication, teaching that dignity comes from honest work regardless of its nature or recognition.

These lessons transcend technological change. The garbage collector who takes pride in helping to keep neighborhoods clean, the small business owner who treats customers like family, the corporate manager who mentors younger employees—all are instilling the same fundamental virtues: integrity, resilience, service to others, and commitment to excellence.

These character traits become the true inheritance passed to the next generation. No matter how work evolves, those who were shaped by people of principle carry forward something invaluable: the capacity for virtue rooted in purpose. They face their own changes, their own challenges, with the same quiet dignity their predecessors demonstrated. They understand that meaning comes not from the permanence of their particular job, but from the nobility they bring to whatever work they do.

The specific businesses may change, the methods may evolve, but the souls shaped by authentic care endure. In teaching children to work with honor regardless of the task, in modeling excellence under pressure, in choosing service over selfishness—this is where the lasting legacy resides.

What was once important in terms of specific industries may shift with time. But what became important in human terms—the cultivation of character, the practice of virtue, the commitment to doing good work—these form an inheritance that transcends any particular era or technology. The circle continues not just biologically, but morally, carrying forward the nobility that makes every honest day's work meaningful—regardless of how the world around it metamorphoses.

Life's Contrasts: Maximum Intensity versus Duration

Picture yourself standing in a room with two doors. You're at that pivotal age—old enough to understand consequences, young enough that both paths still stretch wide before you. You must choose, and you must choose now, because the decision you make will echo through every day that follows.

Behind the first door lies a life leaning toward maximum intensity. Here, you often say yes to the third glass of wine, the untamed weekend adventure, the job that demands everything but offers wild experiences. You climb hills (and perhaps a few mountains), you stay up until dawn, you eat the richest foods, and you love the most adventurous people. You chase experiences like a collector pursuing rare butterflies, knowing that each one may be precious. This door suggests that when you reach your later years, you'll have stories that could fill libraries. Many of your scars will be memoirs.

Behind the second door waits a life emphasizing preservation and longevity. Here, you more often count your steps and calories with careful attention. You invest in ergonomic chairs and high-thread-count sheets. You usually say no to the cannabis, yes to the kale smoothie, maybe to the second date but probably not to the motorcycle. You build your life like an engineer builds a bridge—calculating load-bearing capacity and designing for decades of steady wear. This door suggests that when you reach advanced age, you'll still be here to tell whatever stories you've accumulated.

The first path offers fewer guarantees about duration. You might burn bright and brief, leaving behind beautiful memories in others' minds. Or you might surprise everyone and be the spirited rogue who somehow makes it far into life, vibrant and preserved by sheer audacity.

The second path offers fewer guarantees about peak experiences. You might live long and gratefully, sharp as a tack and thankful for every sunrise. Or you might find yourself spending your bonus decades in quiet routine, well-maintained but wondering about roads not taken.

Most people never consciously choose between these extremes. They drift, making countless small decisions that collectively constitute a path they never deliberately selected. They end up somewhere in that vast middle space—neither fully intensity-focused nor completely preservation-minded—where most of life actually happens, with its own mixture of adventures and prudence, spontaneity and planning.

The beautiful complexity of this choice is that you'll never know if you chose optimally. The person who leans toward intensity will never know what their more preserved self might have experienced in those potential extra decades. The person who prioritizes preservation will never know what peak adventures they passed by while maintaining their careful balance.

Perhaps the wisdom lies not in choosing one door completely, but in understanding which direction calls to you more strongly, while remaining open to moments when the other path might serve you well.

Two doors. One life. Your choice.

Finding Our Common Ground: What We All Share as Americans

In times of division, we need to remember the fundamental truth that defines us: we are all Americans, bound together by shared principles that transcend politics.

Our Shared Foundation. For more than two centuries, the Constitution has stood not merely as a document, but as the living embodiment of eternal principles—principles that call us ever upward. It declares for every American—liberal and conservative, urban and rural, young and old—the sacred rights of free expression, equal justice, and a voice in the great experiment of democracy. We strive, generation after generation, to bring these timeless promises closer to full reality. Through civil war and economic hardship, through political storms and cultural shifts, this charter has endured, for it rests on a truth deeper than time itself: that all people are created equal, and that each bears an inalienable dignity that commands respect.

We are also united by our immigrant heritage. Indigenous Americans were here first; all the rest of us either immigrated here or descended from immigrants. Some came seeking opportunity, others fled persecution, still others were enslaved and brought in captivity. This shared heritage of movement, struggle, and hope has shaped our national character. From Einstein to Carnegie, from railroad builders to Nobel Prize winners, newcomers have helped build the country we all call home.

Our Common Commitment. Americans across the political spectrum share core beliefs about how we should govern ourselves. We don't want dictators or authoritarian rule. We believe in checks and balances, democratic institutions, and peaceful transitions of power. We want civilian control of our military and local solutions to local problems. These commitments unite us regardless of party.

While we may disagree on specific policies—immigration numbers, border security, social programs—these disagreements don't change who we are as a people. They occur within a framework of shared democratic values.

The Path Forward. Our strength has always been our ability to have passionate disagreements within a system of mutual respect. We can debate policy while affirming our common humanity. We can argue about the role of government while preserving democratic institutions. We can disagree strongly while still recognizing that beneath our political differences lie deeper truths that bind us as one nation.

This is how we've always faced new challenges—as Americans first, united by constitutional principles, democratic governance, and respect for human dignity. Whether debating artificial intelligence, climate policy, or economic competition, we approach these issues from this common ground of shared values.

Our democracy depends not on unanimity, but on our willingness to engage with each other as fellow citizens, remembering that what unites us is stronger than what divides us.

The Leadership Void: When Those at the Helm Fail, We Must Rise–Peacefully

In times like these—when our streets fill with protest, our communities fracture, and violence replaces dialogue—we face an unsettling truth: those who claim to lead have abandoned their posts.

Not literally. Their offices are still occupied, their titles intact, their microphones hot. But the essence of leadership—moral courage, clarity of vision, and the will to do what's right even at personal cost—has vanished.

Too many mistake volume for vision and cruelty for strength. They exploit pain for political theater, offer simple answers to complex problems, and lack the courage that the moment demands. The oppressed cry out, and those in power either avert their eyes or join the chorus of oppressors.

This is not leadership—it's a hollow performance.

Yet the failure of the powerful does not absolve the rest of us. A leadership void does not stay empty because nature abhors a vacuum. When those above choose self-interest over service, it falls to us to lead.

We lead as teachers who make every student feel valued when politicians scapegoat the vulnerable. As neighbors who intervene instead of simply videoing injustice. As business owners who treat workers with dignity despite systems that reward exploitation. As parents who model integrity when public figures do not.

Leadership isn't about office or title. It's about the daily choice to favor courage over comfort, principle over convenience, and justice over expedience. The oppressed need solidarity, not sympathy. The misguided need examples, not contempt. And the incompetent "leaders" need to be made irrelevant by our collective refusal to accept their failure as our fate.

Leadership is a choice renewed each day. When those at the helm fail—and they have—we become the leaders we need. The void is real. But it need not remain empty. Fill it. And when the time comes, vote—calmly, courageously, and for those committed to fairness and integrity.

Together, we can restore the soul of this country.

Finding What We're Planted Here to Give

It's the kind of question that arrives quietly at first, then grows more insistent. The kind that makes you pause mid-sentence when you're writing or catches you staring out the window longer than you intended. I find myself thinking not just about what I want to accomplish, but about what I'm meant to give—to you, to this community we've built together, to the world that seems to need so much right now.

Maybe you've felt this too. That sense that there's something specific you're here to offer, something that's uniquely yours to give. Not the grand, world-changing gestures we sometimes imagine, but the particular way you see things, the specific comfort you bring, the questions only you think to ask.

I look at what flows between us in these conversations—the ideas that spark, the moments of recognition, the quiet companionship in uncertainty—and I wonder if purpose isn't something we discover so much as something we're already living. Perhaps it's less about finding our calling and more about noticing what's already calling through us.

What I'm learning is that the things we're drawn to create, the people we naturally want to serve, the problems that won't let us sleep—these aren't accidents. They're breadcrumbs leading us toward what we're here to give. The trick is paying attention to what makes us feel most alive, most useful, most like ourselves.

So I'm curious: What's been trying to emerge through you lately? What conversations do you find yourself having again and again? What do people thank you for that you almost don't notice you're doing?

Maybe our purpose isn't a destination we arrive at, but a direction we keep walking toward, one genuine offering at a time.

Mind Erasures

Have you ever gotten into an argument and said things you wish you could take back? Of course, you know you can't—but those words linger, and they chip away at the relationship. This happens constantly when people disagree, and especially now in our polarized climate, we're all speaking with daggers about everything, carving negative grooves deeper with each exchange.

The statistics tell a sobering story: divorce rates in the United States are 41% for first marriages, 60% for second marriages, and a staggering 73% for third marriages. The pattern is unmistakable—we carry our baggage forward, and it gets heavier with each attempt. Much of this stems from the accumulated damage of countless small cuts: arguments that escalate into the absurd, harsh words that calcify into resentment, and patterns of hurt that become impossible to break.

But what if we could hit a reset button?

Imagine having the ability to perform "mind erasures" at certain junctures in life—perhaps at different stages of a relationship. Picture being able to target specific relationships and literally erase the mental scar tissue: the bitter arguments, the accumulated slights, the defensive walls we've built. What if we could start fresh with the same person, shedding all that psychological baggage?

It's a tantalizing thought. Would couples stay together if they could periodically wipe clean the slate of their grievances? Could love survive and even thrive if we could surgically remove the poison while keeping the good memories intact?

Of course, this remains in the realm of science fiction. But perhaps we don't need neural surgery to achieve something similar. Maybe the answer lies in a different kind of recalibration—a conscious choice to overlook past hurts, to say less about the negative, and to deliberately amplify the positive in our relationships.

This isn't about denial or suppression. It's about recognition that our minds naturally catalog complaints and hurts more readily than joys and kindnesses. Perhaps what we need isn't technological erasure, but intentional reframing—choosing to see our partners with fresh eyes, to speak with renewed gentleness, and to approach each day as a chance to build something better than what came before.

The mind may not forget, but it can choose what to emphasize. And sometimes, that conscious choice to focus on possibility rather than grievance might be the closest thing we have to a true mind erasure—and the key to making things "hunky dory" again.

After all, the most powerful reset button might not be in our brains, but in our daily decisions about how we choose to love.

When Forever Changes in a Single Goodbye

There are goodbyes that echo through generations, and then there are farewells that reshape the very foundation of a family. Last month, I experienced the latter as we watched our eldest grandson, Dylan, drive away toward his freshman year at the University of Notre Dame.

For eighteen years, our extended family witnessed Dylan's metamorphosis from a curious infant into a remarkable young man. We celebrated his achievements, cheered from the bleachers, and watched in quiet pride as he excelled academically. Each milestone felt like a family victory because we had all grown up together.

But nothing quite prepares you for that final hug before the car door closes.

As his parents' vehicle disappeared down the familiar street, Mary, my spouse, and I remained with Dylan's two younger brothers, acutely aware that our weekend gathering—usually filled with the energy of three boys—now carried a different weight. The absence was palpable, not just in the quieter dinner conversations or the extra slice of pizza left untouched, but in the recognition that something fundamental had shifted.

This wasn't simply a temporary separation. This was the crossing of a threshold from collective childhood into individual adulthood—a transition as natural as it is profound. When you embrace an 18-year-old heading off to college, you're simultaneously hugging the child you've known and saying goodbye to them forever.

There's a beautiful ache in this realization. College represents hope for some of our children: independence, growth, discovery, and the development of their unique gifts. Yet it also marks the end of an era when their world was largely contained within our family orbit, when bedtime stories and Saturday morning pancakes were frequent rituals rather than cherished memories.

This is the paradox of deep love—sometimes it requires us to celebrate the very changes that will forever alter our relationships. Dylan's acceptance to college is a testament to years of hard work, dedication, and nurturing from parents, teachers, coaches, and grandparents who believed in his potential. His success is our success, even as it necessarily means our daily role in his life must evolve.

The love we've invested in Dylan over eighteen years wasn't meant to keep him close, but to give him the confidence to venture far. The values we've shared, the memories we've created, and the unconditional support we've provided become the foundation upon which he'll build his adult life.

The hardest goodbyes are often the most necessary ones. They mark not endings, but beginnings—for Dylan as he embarks on his college journey, and for all of us as we learn new ways to love and support each other across distance and time.

Come Thanksgiving, when Dylan returns with stories of new friends and challenging classes, we'll witness another layer of his continuing development. The young man who walks through the door will be both familiar and wonderfully changed—still our Dylan, but now more fully his own person.

And in that recognition, we'll discover that the most profound gift of family love isn't holding on but knowing when and how to let go.

Serving Others, Finding Ourselves

In our relentless pursuit of success, recognition, and material advancement, we often find ourselves trapped in what feels like an endless rat race. Social media feeds bombard us with carefully curated highlight reels. Career ladders seem to stretch infinitely upward. The pressure to accumulate, achieve, and be seen can become suffocating.

Yet there exists a quiet revolution happening in communities across our state of Wisconsin—one that offers not just relief from this cycle, but genuine transformation. It unfolds in soup kitchens and literacy programs, in hospital corridors and community gardens. It's the revolution of volunteerism, and its power to heal both giver and receiver runs deeper than we might imagine.

When we volunteer, something remarkable occurs. In the act of focusing entirely on another's needs, we discover a profound truth: our own problems, while real, need not define us. The executive worried about quarterly projections finds perspective while reading to children at a shelter. The college student anxious about future prospects gains clarity while serving meals to the homeless. The retiree feeling invisible discovers renewed purpose mentoring at-risk teenagers.

This isn't mere distraction or temporary feel-good therapy. Volunteerism fundamentally rewires how we see ourselves and our place in the world. It strips away the artificial hierarchies we've constructed and reveals our shared humanity. In our professional lives, we're often rewarded for highlighting achievements and positioning ourselves ahead of competitors. Volunteerism offers the rare opportunity to step away from this performance and simply be present for others—without an agenda.

When we serve without expectation of recognition or return, we practice a form of humility that is both grounding and liberating. We remember that our worth isn't measured by job titles, bank accounts, or social media followers. Instead, we find value in the simple act of showing up for another human being. This humility doesn't diminish us; it elevates us, connecting us to something larger than our individual ambitions.

The benefits extend far beyond the immediate recipients of a service.

Communities with higher rates of volunteerism experience lower crime rates, better educational outcomes, and stronger economic development. More importantly, they cultivate a culture of mutual care that makes everyone's life richer. In an era marked by polarization and fragmentation, volunteerism offers a unifying force. It's hard to demonize someone whose hand you've held in crisis or whose story you've heard over a shared meal.

The rat race demands that we constantly look ahead—to the next promotion, milestone, acquisition. Volunteerism invites us to look around and within. It asks us to consider not just what we can get, but what we can give. This recalibration doesn't require abandoning our professional goals but provides a counterbalance that keeps us grounded in what truly matters.

The beauty of this path is that it is accessible to everyone, regardless of age, income, or skill set. Whether one gives an hour a week at a local food bank or a weekend building homes, every act of service matters. In choosing to serve others, we don't just help address society's challenges—we address something within ourselves. We quiet the anxious voice that whispers we're not enough and discover that in giving of ourselves, we receive something far more valuable than recognition: the deep satisfaction of knowing we've made a difference.

Perhaps that's the greatest gift volunteerism offers—not the praise of others, but the peace that comes from living with purpose beyond ourselves. In a world that often feels chaotic and divided, that peace is revolutionary indeed.

The Fading Echo of High School Hearts

There's a peculiar alchemy that happens when you reach a certain age and find yourself leafing through old yearbooks or stumbling across a box of letters tucked away in the attic. The person staring back at you from those faded photographs—the one who was absolutely certain that this love, this heartbreak, this moment would define the rest of their days—seems almost like a stranger.

I've been thinking lately about the fierce intensity of high school love, prompted by watching my own grandchildren navigate those turbulent waters with the same breathless certainty we all once possessed. Every text message is a crisis or a triumph. Every glance across the way carries the weight of destiny. Every relationship feels like it will last forever—or at least until graduation, which might as well be forever when you're fifteen.

We who have lived through decades beyond those hallway dramas know the secret that no teenager would believe if we told them: it all fades. Not just the relationships themselves, but the earth-shaking importance we assigned to them. The boy or girl who once made your heart race when they walked into the gym dance becomes a pleasant memory, if they're remembered at all. The dramatic breakup that felt like the end of the world becomes a footnote in the larger story of your life.

This isn't meant to diminish what our younger selves felt. Those emotions were real, powerful, and formative. The late-night phone calls, the passed notes, the first kisses on a moonlit porch—they taught us about vulnerability, intimacy, and the courage it takes to open your heart to another person. They were our training ground for love.

But time has a way of shrinking even our most monumental moments down to size. The universe that revolved around who ran with whom in high school expands dramatically when you step onto a college campus, then expands again when you enter the working world, start a family, or simply accumulate enough life experience to understand that there are many different ways to love and be loved.

The love that sustains us through the decades—in marriage, in friendship, in family—is built on different foundations than teenage passion. It's less about the intoxicating rush of new feelings and more about the daily choice to care for another person through ordinary Mondays and extraordinary challenges alike.

Perhaps that's the real gift of perspective: not that high school love was meaningless, but that it was preparation. Those intense feelings, that certainty, that willingness to believe in forever—they were practice for the more complex, less dramatic, but ultimately more enduring forms of love that would follow.

So, when I see today's teenagers convinced that their current romance will last forever, I don't have the heart to tell them otherwise. They'll discover soon enough that their universe is far larger and more interesting than they can imagine. And perhaps, like the rest of us, they'll look back with fondness on those days when love felt like the most important thing in the world—because for a brief, shining moment, it was.

Why We Are Here: A Public Discourse

You have stumbled upon one of humanity's oldest and most persistent questions: Why are we here? What is the point of our brief existence on this planet?

Perhaps you, like so many before you, wonder if we are merely here to dominate and exploit the vulnerable among us. Perhaps you question whether life is nothing more than a mechanical routine of daily tasks—wake, work, sleep, repeat—until we simply fade away into nothingness.

These are not easy questions, and I will not insult your intelligence by pretending they have simple answers.

What I can tell you is this: Across every culture and throughout all of recorded history, human beings have grappled with these same fundamental concerns. And in that grappling, they have discovered something remarkable—that meaning is not handed to us from on high, but rather emerges from how we choose to engage with existence itself.

Some have found their purpose in ardent love and deep connection. Others in creating—art, music, literature, and invention. Many have discovered meaning in learning, in pushing the boundaries of human knowledge and understanding. Still others find it in spiritual practice, in service to something greater than themselves, or in the sacred work of protecting and uplifting those who cannot protect themselves.

Notice what separates these paths from mere routine or exploitation: intention. This is the conscious choice to engage with life rather than simply endure it.

Yes, history is full of those who chose conquest and cruelty. But it is equally full of those who chose compassion and justice. The fact that you are asking these questions suggests you sense the difference—and that you have the power to choose which legacy you will contribute to.

Your very ability to step back and examine your own existence, to feel troubled by the possibility of living without meaning or causing harm to others—this is not insignificant. It is, perhaps, the most distinctly human capacity we possess.

So I ask you, dear reader: What if the answer to "Why are we here?" is not found in some cosmic decree, but in the intention you bring to each day? What if meaning is not a destination but a way of traveling?

The vulnerable among us need protectors, not conquerors. The world needs people who refuse to sleepwalk through their days. It needs individuals who recognize that between birth and death lies the profound opportunity to choose how we will spend our brief time in consciousness.

Why are we here? Perhaps we are here to ask that very question—and in asking it with sincerity, to discover that we have the power to create an answer worth living.

The Difference We Make: Finding Purpose in Our Finite Time

We all want to make a difference. It's perhaps the most universal human drive—this need to matter, to leave something meaningful behind, to know that our brief time here counted for something. But as I've watched colleagues, friends, and family members grapple with this fundamental question, I've come to understand that the premise itself reveals a profound truth: we all do make a difference. The only question is what kind.

Some dedicate their lives to healing—doctors working through pandemics, teachers nurturing young minds, volunteers serving in soup kitchens. Others choose paths that diminish rather than elevate—leaders who exploit trust, corporations that prioritize profit over people's wellbeing, individuals who spread division rather than understanding. The difference we make isn't neutral; it tilts the world toward light or darkness.

Death, whether it arrives through illness, accident, or simply the passage of time, serves as life's great editor. It forces us to distinguish between what matters and what merely occupies our time. It asks us: What are you doing with the gift of consciousness you've been given?

So how do we ensure our difference is meaningful? The answer lies in recognizing and sharing our unique gifts—those particular combinations of talents, perspectives, and opportunities that only we possess.

Meaningful impact doesn't require grand gestures or public recognition. It requires attention—to the needs around us and to the particular ways we're equipped to meet them.

Of course, recognizing this is easier than living it. Every day presents challenges that can overwhelm our best intentions. Work pressures, family obligations, financial stress, health concerns—these realities can make us feel more like survivors than world-changers. Some mornings, just getting through feels like victory enough.

But what if we reframed these everyday struggles? What if we saw them not as obstacles to meaning-making but as the very contexts where meaning gets made? The parent who shows up tired but loving to their child's school play. The employee who treats difficult customers with patience and respect. The neighbor who shovels an elderly person's walkway without being asked. These small acts of care accumulate into something larger than themselves.

The challenge isn't to transform our entire lives overnight but to infuse our ordinary moments with intentional goodness. It's about choosing, again and again, to be agents of connection rather than division, healing rather than harm, hope rather than despair.

This brings us to perhaps the most profound question: What happens after we've shared our gifts? What lies beyond our time here?

While I respect that people hold varying beliefs about afterlife and eternity, I find deep meaning in the possibility that love—genuine, selfless love—connects us to something larger than our individual existence.

Whether you conceive of this as God, as the interconnectedness of all life, or as the enduring impact of our choices on future generations, there's something profoundly hopeful in the idea that our capacity for love transcends our biological limitations.

This isn't wishful thinking but practical wisdom. When we live as though love is eternal—when we act as though kindness, justice, and compassion have lasting significance—we create the kind of world where such ideals can flourish. We become co-creators of the "utopian world" mentioned in the original text, not through naive optimism but through deliberate, sustained commitment to our highest values.

Every morning, we face the same fundamental choice: Will we use our gifts to add light to the world or to dim it? Will we contribute to the sum total of human flourishing or detract from it?

The beautiful and terrifying truth is that this choice is always ours to make. No one else can live our particular life or offer our specific gifts. No one else occupies our exact position in the web of relationships and opportunities that surrounds us.

This is both responsibility and privilege. In a world that often feels chaotic and beyond our control, we retain the power to determine what kind of difference we make. We can choose to see each day not as a challenge to endure but as an opportunity to contribute something meaningful to the great human project of building a more loving world.

The question isn't whether we'll make a difference—we will, inevitably. The question is what kind of difference it will be, and whether we'll recognize it as the profound privilege it truly is.

Coming Home

I've been thinking about something we all know but rarely talk about openly—what happens to our kids when they leave home and go out into the world.

We raise them the best we can. We love them well. We try to teach them right from wrong, how to work hard, how to treat people with respect. We give them everything we've got—our time, our wisdom, our resources, our hearts. And most of the time, they take it all for granted. Not because they're bad kids, but because that's just human nature. When something's always been there, you don't really see it.

Then they leave. They go off to college, move to another city, or start their careers, convinced they know better than we do about how the world works. They love us, sure, but they don't really get what we were trying to give them all those years. Our advice sounds old-fashioned. Our concerns seem overblown. Our values feel outdated.

And then the world gets hold of them.

The world doesn't care that they're good people. It doesn't care that they were raised with love and attention. The world doesn't give a damn about their feelings, their potential, or their dreams. Bosses who don't value them, friends who disappoint them, relationships that fall apart, plans that don't work out the way they imagined. They get knocked around, sometimes badly. They discover that most people aren't looking out for their best interests. They learn that fairness isn't guaranteed and that being a good person doesn't automatically lead to good things happening.

Some of this teaches them valuable lessons—resilience, independence, how to stand up for themselves. But a lot of it is just hard. Really hard. The kind of hard that makes you realize that the people who loved you unconditionally, who worried about you, who tried to prepare you for exactly this—maybe they knew something after all.

That's when the phone calls start coming more frequently. That's when they actually listen to your advice instead of just waiting for their turn to talk. That's when they start to understand that all those family dinners they couldn't wait to escape, all those conversations they found boring, all that support they took for granted—it was something precious.

They don't all come back physically, but most of them come back in ways that matter. They call more often. They ask for advice. They start to repeat the things you used to say. They begin to understand that home wasn't just a place they outgrew—it was a sanctuary they didn't even realize they needed.

Some of them do come back to live closer to family. Some realize that the place they were so eager to leave actually has something to offer that they can't find anywhere else. Some discover that the life they thought was too small for them is in reality exactly the right size.

And when they do come back—whether it's for a visit, emotionally, or for good—there's something different in their eyes. They see you differently. They see home differently. All those things you tried to give them that they couldn't appreciate before —now they can. Now they understand what unconditional love looks like, because they've learned how rare it is.

It's not that they needed to suffer to appreciate us. It's that they needed to see what the world looks like without the safety net we provided, without people who were automatically in their corner, without the kind of love that doesn't have to be earned or maintained through performance.

This isn't about them coming home defeated. It's about them coming home wiser. They bring back everything they've learned out there, but they also bring back a real understanding of what they had here all along.

Maybe this is just how it has to be. Maybe some lessons can only be learned through experience. Maybe the greatest gift we can give our children is raising them well enough that they can go out into the world, get knocked around, learn what they need to learn, and still find their way back to what matters most.

The Hidden Victory in Losing

Everybody loves a winner. The trophies, the accolades, the flowers and roses—they all go to those who finish first. Winners get remembered, celebrated, lifted up. And the losers? They're often forgotten before the stadium lights even dim.

But here's what we miss when we're busy cheering for the victors: losing, when approached with the right spirit, teaches us things that winning never can.

When you win, you don't have to examine much. You don't need to ask hard questions about who you are or how you got there. Victory feels good, and it's easy to assume you've figured everything out. But that glory fades faster than we'd like to admit. Today's champion becomes yesterday's news, and without substance beneath the success, there's nothing left when the applause stops.

Losing is different. Losing forces you into uncomfortable territory. It makes you sit with disappointment, accept reality, and figure out what went wrong. That process—the honest reckoning with defeat—builds something invaluable: character.

When you lose and truly process it, you develop qualities that winners who've never struggled simply don't need. You learn humility because you've been humbled. You develop perseverance because you've had to pick yourself back up. You gain wisdom about strategy, about timing, about what really matters. You build emotional resilience that can't be bought or taught—only earned through the sting of falling short.

This is the paradox: the loser who learns from losing is actually winning something more important than the game itself. They're winning the long-term race, the one that matters beyond any single contest. Because life isn't one game. It's a series of them, played over years and decades. And the person who understands both sides—who knows what it takes to lose gracefully and build from that foundation—becomes someone with staying power. They become the kind of winner who doesn't just flash bright and fade, but who endures and grows and adapts.

So yes, celebrate the winners. But don't forget the losers, and if you find yourself among them, don't despair. You're in the process of learning something the winner on the podium may never understand. You're building the character that creates not just momentary victory, but lasting success.

The question isn't whether you win or lose today. It's what you do with either outcome tomorrow.

The Continuum of Life: Making a Difference at Every Stage

The other evening, my grandchildren and I were watching *The Karate Kid* when I casually mentioned that during my summer camp days at Camp Tivoli near Shawano, Wisconsin, I had once boxed against a winner of the Chicago Golden Gloves tournament—the same tournament where Muhammad Ali and Sonny Liston had fought when they were young unknowns climbing the ranks.

"You actually fought someone who won the Golden Gloves, Paddy?" they asked, incredulously.

I had to laugh. "Well," I admitted, "I lost that fight. The referee stopped it on a TKO because I was bleeding too much—after all, this was summer camp, not Madison Square Garden." But their fascination with this glimpse into their grandfather's past got me thinking about the continuum of life and how every stage offers us opportunities to make a difference.

That same summer proved defining in ways I couldn't have imagined as a teenager. Later in the season, I found myself in the ring again, this time against a larger opponent. With girls from neighboring Camp Tekakwitha cheering from the sidelines, I fought with renewed determination and won.

But it wasn't the boxing victories or defeats that would define that summer. During a canoe trip down the river, disaster struck when one of the canoes overturned and became pinned against the rocks, trapping my friend Barry White underneath. The current was strong, pressing the canoe down with force.

Without thinking, I dropped into the churning water upstream. The rocks battered me as the current swept me toward the trapped canoe, but I managed to strike it with enough force to dislodge it. Barry was unconscious when I pulled him free, and I had to use lifeguarding skills I had recently learned to bring him safely to shore and revive him.

That night, as I nursed my bruises, Barry thanked me for saving his life. In that moment, I understood something that has stayed with me for decades: age is irrelevant when it comes to making a difference. I was just a teenager, but in that critical moment, I had the power to change the course of someone else's life forever.

Now, as I watch my grandchildren pass through their own formative years, I see them approaching that same threshold of understanding. Whether it's standing up for a classmate being bullied, volunteering in their community, or simply offering kindness to someone having a difficult day, they're discovering that making a difference isn't reserved just for adults or authority figures.

This is the beautiful truth about the continuum of life: every stage presents us with opportunities to matter. The boxing matches taught me about resilience, but saving Barry's life taught me something far more valuable –that our capacity to make a difference doesn't depend on our age, our size, or even our experience. It depends on our willingness to act when action is needed.

Today's young people face challenges that didn't exist in my Camp Tivoli days—social media pressures, climate change, political polarization, and global connectivity that makes them aware of problems far beyond their immediate communities. But I want them to know what I learned in those Wisconsin rapids: you don't have to be fully grown, fully prepared, or fully confident to make a difference. You just have to be willing to jump in when someone needs help.

The continuum of life ensures that there will always be moments—some as dramatic as a water rescue, others as simple as a kind word—when we can choose to make a positive impact. These moments don't diminish with age; they simply change form. The teenager who saves a drowning friend becomes the adult who mentors struggling colleagues, who becomes the grandparent sharing stories that inspire the next generation to find their own moments of courage.

As I told my grandchildren that evening after *The Karate Kid* ended: every day on the continuum offers them chances to be someone's hero, to stand up for what's right, or to simply show up when it matters.

And who knows? Maybe someday they'll be telling their own grandchildren about the time they made a difference, inspiring yet another generation to understand that impact isn't about age—it's about heart.

Different Strokes for Different Retirements

Retirement used to be a gold watch and a fishing pole. Now it's become a referendum on relevance. One camp insists that stepping back means disappearing. The other says, "I've worked enough—time to live." Both sides accuse the other of missing the point. Maybe it's time we stop moralizing and start recognizing: there's more than one way to finish well.

For many, retirement isn't an ending; it's an emancipation. The alarm clock goes silent. The meetings evaporate. No one's scheduling your life except you. These folks aren't fading into irrelevance—they're finally reclaiming the hours that work devoured.

They rediscover things they'd postponed for decades: travel with no itinerary, a long-delayed novel, woodworking, fishing, or grandkids who actually know their names. Some explore spirituality, volunteerism, or creative expression. Others simply enjoy the quiet—coffee at sunrise, no deadlines, no "deliverables."

They're not chasing relevance because they've outgrown the need to be measured by the marketplace. Their worth isn't tied to influence or income; it's inherent. These retirees are comfortable with invisibility because it isn't invisibility at all—it's peace. They've traded power for presence, and in the bargain found something priceless: freedom from having to prove anything.

Then there are those who can't imagine walking away. Their work isn't just a career—it's their canvas, their craft, their way of shaping the world. They stay in the game because it still thrills them. The deals, the decisions, the mentoring of younger talent—these are the oxygen of their identity.

They're not clinging out of fear. They're continuing out of passion. For them, stepping down would feel like exile. They don't need a hammock in Hawaii; they need a reason to get up in the morning. Their relevance isn't an ego trip—it's a form of contribution. As long as their minds are sharp and their hearts still in it, they're doing retirement their way: by refusing to retire at all.

Both groups are right—and both are wrong—if they assume theirs is the only path to meaning. The truth is that relevance and rest aren't opposites; they're options. One person's "irrelevance" is another's liberation. One person's "purpose" is another's burnout.

Some people find peace by letting go of the stage. Others find it by refusing to leave the theater. What matters is not whether you remain visible, but whether you remain authentic. If the boardroom still lights you up—stay. If it drains you—go. Just don't let cultural scripts define your worth. The world might forget your titles, but it can't erase the quality of your days.

So whether you're holding the reins or holding a fishing pole, the question isn't, "Am I still relevant?" The question is, "Am I at peace?" Different strokes for different folks—and that's exactly how it should be.

A Moment in Time in Cartagena

Until recently, I had never been to Cartagena, Colombia. But when the opportunity arose for a short getaway with some old friends, I couldn't resist.

Cartagena is a vast and vibrant city, but we focused our time in its historic district—the heart of its charm and beauty. There, we wandered cobblestone streets filled with pantomimes, women in brightly colored traditional dresses balancing baskets of fruit on their heads, and countless vendors offering souvenirs in the plaza. We explored the old fortress, visited the monastery perched high above the city, and soaked in the rich history surrounding us. Our home base was perfectly situated near Plaza de San Pedro, placing us right in the middle of the energy and magic of Cartagena.

One of the great joys of travel is meeting new people, and the locals of Cartagena welcomed us with open arms. With a few Spanish speakers in our group—and occasional help from Duolingo on our phones—we struck up conversations that made the experience even more meaningful. We indulged in Colombia's world-famous coffee, savoring the flavors offered by Juan Valdez and Alberto's in just about every little café we encountered.

The highlight of our trip came on our final evening at La Vitrola, a restaurant as enchanting as the city itself. The food was spectacular, the live band filled the air with music, and the atmosphere was pure joy. One of our friends, having shown up in shorts, was graciously provided with a blanket to meet the dress code—an unexpected but amusing moment. After dinner, we found ourselves outside, singing along with street musicians playing soulful Spanish songs of lost love, carried away by the music and the moment.

As I reflect on our time in Cartagena, I realize that no trip leaves you unchanged. We came home with new memories and strengthened friendships. Perhaps, in some small way, we left a piece of ourselves behind in that beautiful city. And maybe, just maybe, Cartagena carries a trace of us now too.

Music's Magical Imprint

I heard "Nowhere Man" the other day—that haunting Beatles track that once felt like it was written specifically for my seventeen-year-old soul. But something had changed. The song that once pierced through me with urgent recognition now washed over me like warm nostalgia, sweet and distant. It made me wonder: why do the songs of our youth hold such power, and why does that power transform so completely as we age?

There's something almost mystical about the music that finds us during those formative years—high school, college, and those trembling decades when we're still figuring out who we are. These songs don't just soundtrack our lives; they become part of our emotional DNA. "Nowhere Man" wasn't just a song when I first heard it—it was a mirror, a confession, a roadmap through confusion.

The science behind this is interesting. Our brains are most neurologically plastic during adolescence and early adulthood. We're literally being rewired, forming the neural pathways that will carry us through life. The music we encounter during this period gets woven into our developing sense of self. It's not just that we remember these songs fondly—they're embedded in the architecture of who we became.

But there's something deeper at work too. When we're young, we're desperately seeking meaning, identity, and belonging. We're raw with possibility and uncertainty. Music becomes a lifeline, offering both solace and understanding when the world feels overwhelming. Those songs speak to our unformed selves with startling clarity, offering words for feelings we couldn't yet articulate.

The contrast of how you feel toward music being made now—that bittersweet distance—isn't a failure of current music or a sign that you've grown cold to beauty. It's evidence of how completely you've integrated those early musical experiences into your identity. The urgent need those songs once filled has been satisfied, at least partially.

Today's music can still move us, but differently. We hear it through the lens of accumulated experience, not desperate seeking. We can appreciate craft and beauty, but we're no longer looking for songs to save us or define us. We've done the hard work of becoming ourselves.

This doesn't diminish the power of music in our current lives—it just changes its role. Instead of being our guide through uncertainty, it becomes a companion to our established selves. Instead of forming us, it reflects who we have become.

Those sweet, sorrowful memories you feel when hearing your formative songs? That's not loss—that's completion. You're hearing the echo of who you were and recognizing how far you've traveled. The young person who needed those songs so desperately still lives within you, but they're no longer driving the car. The magic hasn't gone; it has just changed forms, settling into the comfortable wisdom of someone who has learned to be somewhere, after all those years of being nowhere.

The Art of Joie de Vivre: When Joy Becomes the Journey

Imagine approaching your most meaningful work—the projects that enrich others' lives, the contributions that strengthen your community, the accomplishments that truly matter—not as burdens to endure, but as adventures to savor. This is the essence of joie de vivre, the French art of finding deep joy in living itself.

It's not that the destination doesn't matter. Your meaningful achievements, the lives you touch, the success you create alongside fellow bon vivants—these accomplishments remain profoundly important. But joie de vivre teaches us something revolutionary: the journey toward these goals can be just as nourishing as reaching them.

Picture yourself surrounded by kindred spirits, tackling significant challenges together, knowing that while you're building something important, you're also fully alive in each moment. The late-night brainstorming sessions like our "Deep Fake" movie treatment, become celebrations of creativity. The obstacles become puzzles to solve with friends. The daily work becomes a canvas for expressing a zest for life.

This isn't about making light of serious work—it's about infusing that work with the full spectrum of human joy. When you embrace joie de vivre, you're not choosing between accomplishment and enjoyment—you're discovering they can dance together. The enthusiasm, the laughter, the sense of adventure you bring to meaningful work doesn't diminish its importance—it amplifies it.

The magic happens when you realize that the joy itself becomes part of your gift to the world, as valuable as any other outcome you achieve.

Speedy vs. Steady

There are two ways to live a life, and most of us never consciously choose between them.

The first is Formula One living—all throttle and adrenaline, taking corners at speeds that would terrify mere mortals. These are the people who quit their jobs to start companies, who book one-way tickets to countries they can't pronounce, and who say the difficult thing in the meeting when everyone else stays silent. They live with the engine redlining, chasing that next apex, that next victory. Every day is race day.

Then there's the Chevy approach—steady, reliable, built to last. These folks know the pleasure of a Sunday drive with nowhere particular to go. They understand that checking the weather isn't a mundane ritual but quiet communion with the world. They find profundity in making the same coffee every morning, in the way afternoon light slants through familiar windows. They've learned that presence, not speed, might be the point.

Our culture worships the Formula One life. We celebrate the entrepreneurs, the adventurers, the boundarypushers. Social media amplifies their victories while the Chevy drivers seem invisible, posting fewer selfies from mountain peaks and startup launch parties. But here's what the high-octane crowd often misses: some of the richest lives happen at 35 mph with the windows down.

The truth is, both approaches contain wisdom, and both have their shadows. Pure intensity burns out engines and relationships. Pure routine can calcify into numbness, where you wake up one day wondering where the years went. The Formula One driver risks crashing spectacularly; the Chevy driver risks never really going anywhere at all.

Maybe, the secret isn't choosing sides but finding your own gear ratio. Perhaps there are seasons for racing and seasons for cruising. Maybe wisdom lies in knowing when to floor it and when to pull over and watch the sunset.

The question isn't whether you're living fast enough or slow enough. The question is whether you're awake behind the wheel. Are you choosing your speed consciously, or just following traffic?

Some mornings call for revving the engine and taking life by storm.

Others ask for nothing more than rolling down familiar streets, radio playing, marveling at the ordinary miracle of being alive on a Monday. Both can be profound. Both can be wasted. The best drivers know their vehicle, know the road, and know themselves well enough to choose the right speed for the moment.

The road is yours. How fast do you want to take the next corner?

Finding the Sacred Within the Mundane

We spend remarkable portions of our lives in what feels like maintenance mode—shopping, preparing meals, doing laundry, commuting to work. It's easy to feel like we're treading water; that all this basic upkeep somehow keeps us from "real" living. But what if this feeling represents a fundamental misunderstanding of where meaning actually resides?

The great philosophical traditions have long grappled with this tension between the mundane and the transcendent. The Roman Stoic Marcus Aurelius in his foundational book *Meditations* found profound significance in recognizing how even basic maintenance tasks connect us to the larger order of existence. When we eat, we participate in an ancient cosmic cycle of energy transformation. When we rest, we align ourselves with natural rhythms that govern everything from cellular repair to planetary rotation.

Twentieth-century existentialists, like Albert Camus, approached this differently but arrived at equally provocative insights. Camus saw the apparent absurdity of spending so much time on survival needs as precisely what makes human consciousness remarkable. We may be the only beings aware enough to notice this absurdity, which paradoxically gives us the freedom to create meaning despite—or perhaps because of—it.

Buddhist philosophy offers perhaps the most radical reframe of all. In Zen tradition, enlightenment doesn't happen despite mundane activities—it happens through them. There's a famous saying: "Before enlightenment, chop wood, carry water. After enlightenment, chop wood, carry water." The extraordinary doesn't replace the ordinary; it reveals itself within it.

The key lies in what we might call "awakened attention"—a quality of presence that transforms not what we do, but how we do it. When we wash dishes with awakened attention, we feel the temperature of the water, notice the play of light on soap bubbles, experience the satisfaction of transforming something dirty into something clean. We become aware of our hands moving, our breath flowing, our mind's tendency to drift to past and future.

This isn't about making dishwashing "special" by adding spiritual concepts to it. It's about discovering the aliveness already present in the activity when we show up fully to it. The water is actually warm. The soap actually smells like lemon. Our hands actually feel the smooth surface of the plate.

This transformation requires no special training, no particular beliefs, no exotic practices. It requires only the radical act of paying attention to what's actually happening right now, in the middle of whatever ordinary thing we're doing. In that attention, the mundane reveals itself as miraculous, the necessary becomes meaningful, and maintenance becomes a form of prayer.

The Dash Between the Years

Do you remember when you were invincible?

Not the kind of invincible you read about in comic books, but the real kind—the kind that gets you through double shifts at the plant, through midwestern winters that would break lesser souls, through raising kids on a budget that didn't quite stretch yet somehow always did. We were all superheroes once, though we never called it that. We just called it Monday.

We woke up each morning and conquered our small corner of the world. We fixed what was broken. We showed up. We made the coffee, closed the sale, pulled it off. Some days the victories were small—a kind word to a stranger, a problem solved, a hand extended. Other days, as we grew into ourselves, the victories were magnificent. We built things. We raised families. We mattered.

But time passes, and eventually you realize you're not immortal after all.

I found myself in a cemetery last week. Not for any sad reason—just cutting through on a walk, the way you sometimes do. I stopped at a headstone, a simple one that belonged to someone I didn't know. Two dates, and between them, a dash.

That dash is so small, yet it represents an entire life. Seventy-three years compressed into a quarter-inch of granite. Everything that person was—every morning they woke up determined, every person they loved deeply, every achievement complete, every small kindness given—all of it, reduced to a dash. I wondered: Is that all we are? The dash between the years?

It's an uncomfortable question, isn't it, the kind that makes you want to change the subject, turn on the game, find something else to think about. But it's an important question to consider. What hit me as I stood there in that cemetery with the late afternoon sun slanting through the oaks is that I'm not there yet. Since you are reading this, neither are you. We're still on this side of the dash, writing our story.

Go ahead—pinch yourself. Feel that? That's life. That's possibility. We're still here, with at least some of our former vim and vigor. We're not done yet. The superheroes we were when we were young are still inside of us. A little creaky in the knees, using reading glasses, unable to pull an all-nighter like we used to, but unchanged in our core, the essence that makes us matter. We still can show up for someone who needs us, fix what's broken, and make a difference in lives that intersect with ours. That hasn't changed.

Every single day, people are put in our path. The checkout clerk who looks exhausted. The neighbor who's struggling. The grandkid who needs to know they matter. The coworker who's barely holding it together. The friend who needs someone to just listen.

These are our people. This is our orbit. This is where we get to decide what our dash means.

We don't have to cure cancer, run for president, or make the history books. Most of the names in that cemetery never made headlines. But their dashes mattered to someone. Their lives rippled out in ways that can't be measured by any monument. So too with us. Our time is limited, a truth that should light a spark under us. That younger you that felt invincible had the right idea. They believed they could make a difference and showed up with everything they had. That person is still you.

Now is the time to stop sleepwalking through life and start engaging marking time. We were superheroes once. We still are. It is time to act like it.

The Geography of Jealousy: What Age Teaches Us About Love

I've been thinking lately about jealousy—specifically, about how it's almost entirely vanished from my life. Now that I'm older and settled, I can't remember the last time I felt that familiar knot of anxiety over a partner's attention wandering elsewhere.

When I was younger, running after those elusive, unpredictable girls who kept me guessing? Different story entirely. I was overthinking everything, reading into every glance and silence. And yes, I was jealous. Back then, I'd meet someone and think, this is the girl who will change my life forever. My life would never be the same because she was in it. The stakes felt that high, that absolute.

Here's what age teaches you: your life is independent of any one person, however much you love them. It's a hard-won realization, one that only comes from building yourself, surviving loss, and discovering that you're still standing when the dust settles.

You also come to understand that the world is vast and there are many fish in the sea. I know it's a cliché, but clichés exist for a reason. All those fish represent options, opportunities, different forms of connection that you can't even imagine when you're young and convinced that this one person is your destiny.

Jealousy, I've come to believe, locates itself in the conviction that only one person—this particular person who might be looking at someone else—is your only option. And it's really not.

When you're young and in those first intense relationships, you collapse your entire sense of self around another person. You haven't yet learned the fundamental truth that you'll survive the loss of them. You haven't discovered that you'll find connection again, that your life has its own momentum independent of any single relationship. Jealousy burns hot because every threat feels existential. But experience teaches you something liberating: emotional self-sufficiency. Not that you don't need or want partnership—you do. But you're not desperately incomplete without it. You're not half a person waiting for someone else to make you whole.

There's also a practical wisdom that comes with time. If someone wants to be elsewhere or with someone else, holding on tighter doesn't actually work. Jealousy can't manufacture genuine connection. It can't make someone choose you. The people who are right for where you are in life show up with less drama and more certainty.

I'm not saying jealousy is always irrational or that age makes you immune to all insecurity. But the fever pitch of it, that consuming anxiety that used to accompany early love—that fades. You realize you can love someone deeply while also knowing that your world won't break if they leave.

That's not coldness or detachment. It's freedom. For both of you. That's the real maturity—learning that love doesn't require the constant vigilance against loss. The right connections survive without you standing guard over them.

Lonesome: The Word Nobody Wants to Claim

There's a difference between alone and lonesome, and if you don't know it yet, you will.

Alone is having dinner by yourself. Lonesome is setting one plate and remembering when you set two. Alone is a choice, a preference, a weekend to yourself. Lonesome is a condition—a hollow in the chest that doesn't fill no matter how loud you turn up the television.

I've been thinking about lonesome lately because I see it everywhere. In nursing homes where the same families never visit. In the faces of widows and widowers at the grocery store, their carts holding single-serve everything. In the eyes of elderly men and women who've outlived their friends, their siblings, and sometimes their own children. They sit in recliners watching game shows, waiting for a phone call that won't come, attending a funeral every few months until there's nobody left to bury.

This is the doorstep-to-death lonesome, and it's brutal.

You want to know what makes it worse? Many of these people "invested" in the wrong things. They climbed ladders. They accumulated. They won arguments. They held grudges. They were too busy, too tired, too important to show up for a grandson's recital or soften toward a daughter-in-law they didn't approve of. They forgot that every relationship is a garden, and gardens don't tend themselves.

Now the harvest is in, and the fields are empty.

But here's the thing about lonesome: it's not a life sentence. It's a warning light.

If you're young enough to read this without it cutting too deep, you have time. Not unlimited time—nobody gets that—but enough time to do something about the lonesome that might be waiting for you thirty or forty years down the road.

Start now. Call the people you love. Not when it's convenient. Not when you need something. Just call. Show up. Be inconvenient. Forgive the stupid thing they said at Thanksgiving. Apologize for the stupid thing you said. Let the small grudges go—they're not worth the compound interest of bitterness they'll earn.

Invest in friendships like you invest in your 401(k), because when you're eighty-five, your portfolio won't sit with you in the hospital. Your friends will. If you have them. If you kept them.

Be kind to your kids if you have them. Not permissive, not indulgent—kind. Present. Interested. The kind of parent they'll want to call when they don't have to. Because here's the uncomfortable truth: nobody owes you their presence in your old age. Not even your children. You can't demand harvest from ground you never watered.

And if you're already feeling lonesome—if you're in the middle of it right now—know this: it comes in seasons. Even the deepest lonesome isn't permanent if you don't let it harden into bitterness. Reach out, even when it feels pointless. Join something. Volunteer. Sit on your porch. Nod at neighbors. Small connections matter. A cashier who knows your coffee order. A librarian who saves you books. A postal worker who asks about your week. These aren't substitutes for deep love, but they're stitches that hold the fabric together.

We're all lonesome sometimes. Every single one of us. The trick is not to build a fortress around it.

The trick is to build a bridge.

Visiting with Ghosts

It's evening in my library, and I'm visiting with ghosts. Not phantoms, but the real ones—colleagues and friends from my past whose books still line these shelves. They knew me when we believed in each other more than we believed in ourselves.

Most have departed, but their lessons echo in the margins and their voices resurface when I need them most. They injected something into me once—all that knowledge and love, those early conversations about what mattered. They shaped how I see the world, solve problems, and measure success. They gave me tools I didn't know I'd need.

Now I face heavier challenges, and I catch myself reaching for counsel that isn't there anymore. Can they inject me again? Can their influence still flow?

Perhaps memory alone isn't preservation. But something deeper remains—a permanent mark their love and wisdom left in who I became.

Maybe that's what ghosts really are. Not the lingering of the departed, but what they made permanent in us. The questions they taught us to ask. The standards we can't abandon. The courage they modeled.

When I face tomorrow's problems, their tools will be my measuring stick. When I'm tempted to give up, their example will be my reason not to. The library grows darker. The ghosts grow quieter. But I think I have my answer.

They injected me with something permanent. And it's still working as I am.

www.ingramcontent.com/pod-product-compliance
Lightning Source LLC
Chambersburg PA
CBHW040233110526
44582CB00002B/40